THE DOG WHISPERER

PRESENTS

GOOD HABITS FOR GREAT DOGS

THE DOG WHISPERER

PRESENTS

GOOD HABITS FOR GREAT DOGS

A Positive Approach to Solving Problems for Puppies and Dogs

Paul Owens

Bestselling author of The Dog Whisperer *and* The Puppy Whisperer

with Norma Eckroate

adamsmedia
Avon, Massachusetts

Published by Adams Media, a division of F+W Media, Inc.
57 Littlefield Street
Avon, MA 02322
www.adamsmedia.com

ISBN 10: 1-4405-0321-4
ISBN 13: 978-1-4405-0321-4

Library of Congress Cataloging-in-Publication Data
is available from the publisher.

Printed in the United States of America.
J I H G F E D C B A

This publication is designed to provide accurate and authoritative information with regard to the subject matter covered. It is sold with the understanding that the publisher is not engaged in rendering legal, accounting, or other professional advice. If legal advice or other expert assistance is required, the services of a competent professional person should be sought.
　　—From a *Declaration of Principles* jointly adopted by a Committee of the American Bar Association and a Committee of Publishers and Associations

Many of the designations used by manufacturers and sellers to distinguish their product are claimed as trademarks. Where those designations appear in this book and Adams Media was aware of a trademark claim, the designations have been printed with initial capital letters.

Photos on pages 39; 99; 100; 123; 124; 125; 129; 177; 178; 180; 181; 183; 191; 192; 206; 207; 208; and "look and "down" photos on page 79 by Brain Stemmler of Stemmler Photography

Photos on pages viii; 41; 42; 53; 54; 86; 90; 91; 92; 94; 95; 104; 106; 121; 126; 127; 128; 170; 201; 202; and "bed," "toy," and "sit" photos on page 79 by Erin Tomanek of Paw Prints Pet Portraiture

Illustrations on pages 25; 79; 155; and 159 by Francis Sporer

Illustration of "Betty" on pages 9; 57; 117; and 157 by Jacci Stincic

Photos on pages 188 and 189 by Marianne Goebel

Photos on pages 38; 75; 76; and "look" and "down" photos on page 79 by Harvey Branman of Photography As An Art

Illustration of Gentle Leader head collar on page 39 used with permission of Premier Pet Products

This book is available at quantity discounts for bulk purchases.
For information, please call 1-800-289-0963.

Contents

Acknowledgments

There are many people who assisted greatly in the process of creating this book. We're grateful to everyone at Adams Media, especially our editor, Meredith O'Hayre; copyeditor, Carol Goff; the Adams graphics team; and also to our wonderful agent, Lisa Hagan.

We're grateful to our photographers, whose professionalism and patience are incomparable: Erin Tomanek at Paw Prints Pet Portraiture, Brian Stemmler at Stemmler Photography, and Harvey Branman at Photography as an Art. And thanks to Bob Tomanek for his help at the photo shoot.

Special thanks to our terrific graphic designer, Francis Sporer, who has a unique ability to put form to concepts and beautifully conveyed our message in the four illustrations he created specifically for this book.

For their generous gifts of time and valuable input on the manuscript, our special thanks to Andrea Sholer, Arita Trahan, and Dorna Sakurai.

Some people always step up to the plate and say yes. For their longtime support and generosity of spirit, Barbara Holiday and Dave Reintz, and dog trainer extraordinaire, Nicole Wilde, will always be among the saints in our world.

Annette Leahy is a webmaster extraordinaire with her talents of both technological wizardry and expert writing. Thanks for the peace of mind that you bring, knowing that you are on the job for us.

Special thanks to those friends whose furry sidekicks came out to strut their stuff for the photographs in this book and demonstrate how it is done: Joan and Lauren Asarnow with sweet Layla; Barbara Holiday and Dave Reintz with the amazing Bozley the Beagle; Bill Marquardt and his wonderful dog, Ike; and Carol Cupp with the fabulous Rocket; the Newcombe Family and the awesome Jack; and Jane Wiedlin and Orbit, the queen of the universe.

In addition, Paul would especially like to thank the Owens clan: Pam, Peg, Pat and Tom, Jennifer Mielziner, Jenina Schutter, Jim and Keelin O'Neill, and the blessed Molly and Grady. Your support and faith made it all possible.

And blessings to my awesome coauthor and friend Norma Eckroate whose incomparable writing skills and otherworldly insight and talent transforms even the most tangled, bird's-nest of a phrase into profound prose. Sincere gratitude and appreciation as it was truly an honor and a great ride.

Lastly, special thanks to Terry Cranendonk, dog trainer extraordinaire, for his friendship, consideration, support, and contributions, especially to the chapter on play. Great stuff and greatly honored and appreciated.

Imagine.

Whatever we can imagine we can make real.

So imagine a smile on your face, a hitch in your giddy-up, and a little peace in your heart.

Look into those eyes and say,

"We're in this together, pal. Whatever the problem, no matter how long it takes, we'll work it out. And we'll have fun doing it."

And then you do.

Introduction

This is the world's only self-help book for both you and your puppy or dog. Dogs learn to get what they want by their own actions, just as we humans learn how to get what we want by our own actions.

In this book, you'll learn how you can easily create good new habits that will lead to your dog forming good habits and more reliable behavior. No matter where you are on the training continuum—whether you just brought your first puppy or dog home or have a dog who already does some basic behaviors—this new habit training method will fine-tune and empower your training and dogspeak skills.

Habit training fast-tracks dog training because it focuses on making education a natural, everyday process. Training becomes fun rather than a chore. And by using this method, problems like jumping, begging at the table, pulling on walks, etc. are easily resolved. With the step-by-step instructions offered in this book, you'll find that habit training is the quickest way to reach any goal and get ourselves and our dogs to do what we want them to do. Habits rule!

This book also addresses the three major issues every problem-ridden, dog-human family deals with: not knowing what to do, not being motivated to do it, and not having the willpower to follow through. By applying the suggestions presented in this book, you will quickly and easily:

🦴 Learn how to teach yourself and your dog what to do and how to do it;

⌓ Learn how to motivate both you and your dog so both of you get greater enjoyment in working together and become one big happy family;

⌓ Learn how to develop the willpower to continue the process until you've reached your goals.

This book places a heavy emphasis on play and games. Everyone enjoys playing with their dogs but many people don't realize how important play and having fun can be in teaching dogs to be reliable. Play gets what you want without the hassle of long, formal training sessions or feeling like you're competing with your dog.

One of the most unusual and exciting aspects of this book is the Seven-Day Vacation for Canine Education program. During this "vacation period" you will *not* ask your dog to sit, lie down, heel, get his toy, go to his spot, come, or stay. No vocal or hand signals of any kind are to be used, except for those needed to play some games, such as Find It, Tug, and Fetch. This unique and powerful program supercharges one's ability to "speak dog." It makes training so easy and effective that it's impossible not to see immediate results.

Another unique aspect of this book is access to an online video that all readers get for free. This video allows readers to see habit training methods in action and clearly demonstrates the effectiveness and power of these methods. You can access it at *www.DogWhispererDVD.com/habits*.

Habit training employs the same principles of positive, nonviolent training methods and compassionate leadership presented in my earlier books. Dr. Martin Luther King once was asked why he didn't use physical confrontation and violence in his battle for freedom, he replied, "If peace is our goal, then our means must be peaceful." This book advocates and promotes that philosophy in raising and training our dogs. You become a life coach for your dog, keeping him and all things around him safe while teaching him what it is you want him to do. It's all about having fun and using positive, nonviolent discipline.

Positive training stresses the importance of using scientific principles, rooted in kindness, to set rules and behavioral boundaries for your dog. This is done by learning how to step-by-step correct your dog's behavior rather than correct your dog.

In short, this book will help get you and your dog on the path for a lifetime of peace, health, and happiness in the home.

Part 1

Habit Training and Why It Works

Chapter 1

Creating New Habits That Become Powerful Dog Training Tools

Training the family dog can often become a vicious cycle starting with the stress of feeling that the dog's not listening to what you're saying which, over time, creates more stress. It's almost as if there's a competition going on between you and your dog, and as a result the dog listens even less, and the stress increases even more for both of you. And on and on.

Dogs are supposed to help relieve stress, not add to it. But after a while the chewed slippers, the jumping, the barking, the not-coming-when-called get to be a little much. So we spend millions of dollars each year on dog training classes, books, and DVDs. After all this, it's not unusual for people to finally just give up and give in. And training comes to a halt. Why? Because:

🦴   The training is too hard to fit into a busy lifestyle.

🦴   It's easier to just live with it.

🦴 Training is too expensive.

🦴 Training doesn't work.

🦴 People think their dog is too old or too dumb.

To help people resolve the seemingly irreconcilable issues they have with their beloved family dog so everyone can live happily ever after, dog trainers are always on the lookout for something to make training easier to understand and simpler to do. The easier and the simpler it is, the more motivated people will be to actually do it.

For over thirty-five years, in addition to being a professional dog trainer, I have also practiced and taught yoga and stress management. These two careers have offered a unique perspective on both humans and dogs. A couple of years ago, the thought hit me that people might be much more likely to spend time training their dogs and have fun doing it if they didn't *think* about training but simply made it part of their everyday life. In other words, if training becomes a habit rather than a chore—it all becomes really easy. Getting ready for work is not a chore, it's a habit. You brush your teeth, you comb your hair, you wash your body the same way every day. Eating meals is not a chore, it is a habit. Driving your car is a habit, punching the buttons in the elevator is a habit, checking your e-mails is a habit, and taking your dog out to eliminate is a habit. Most people don't think of these things as work, they are simply everyday routines. Training your dog can also become a routine and, if it does, you create a relationship that flows instead of a relationship that percolates with friction.

So sailing through life with your dog all has to do with simply forming the right habits.

Occasionally I meet people with very well trained dogs who had *no* formal training. They never read a book, watched a DVD, attended a group dog training class, or had a professional trainer visit their home. Yet their dogs seemed well-mannered and well-adjusted. It's pretty evident these people developed a great rapport with their dogs and intuitively did the type of habit training that this book is about. They are shining examples of how being connected with your dog creates camaraderie and a peaceful, fun, and harmonious relationship. Through habit training, everyone can develop even greater rapport with their dog while, at the same time, shaping great behaviors.

There are two ways that you'll incorporate habit training—through habits that *you* adopt and habits that you encourage *your dog* to adopt. First, let's look at how new human habits can solve a problem:

Using New Human Habits to Solve a Problem

Behavior Problem: Your dog bolts out the door whenever you open it.

Your Bad Habit: Not checking to see where your dog is before you open the door. Because of your bad habit, your dog developed the bad and dangerous habit of bolting out the door as soon as it opens.

Your New Habit: To solve the problem, replace your bad habit with a new and better one. Every time you put your hand on the doorknob, get in the habit of turning around to make sure your dog is a safe distance from the door before you open it.

You are training *yourself* to do something very simple. Within twenty-eight days, you will find yourself automatically checking to see where your dog is before opening the door. And just this one simple new habit could literally save your dog's life.

Following the same process, the problem can also be solved if your dog forms a new habit.

Using New Dog Habits to Solve a Problem

Behavior Problem: Your dog bolts out the door whenever you open it.

Your Dog's Bad Habit: Responding to the trigger of the door being opened.

Your Dog's New Habit: By asking your dog to sit whenever you put your hand on the doorknob and stay when the door opens, what's going to happen? He will soon make this behavior habitual. Within twenty-eight days, following the steps outlined in this book, he will automatically sit whenever your hand touches the doorknob and stay there when the door opens without you having to say a word. Then it's a just a matter of strengthening this habit over time.

How easy was that? By consistently repeating a sequence of actions over a short period time, you'll be able to safely open the door, knowing that your dog is happily sitting there instead of bolting out the door. (In Chapter 11, you'll learn how to teach your dog to sit and do other basic behaviors.)

Here's another problem solver: If your dog runs to the window and barks every time the mail carrier comes up the walk, you can teach your dog the replacement habit of going to his bed whenever the mail carrier appears. This will give the dog something else to do instead of habitually "protecting the home." Within twenty-eight days, the go-to-your-bed behavior will become your dog's new habit. Every time the mail carrier shows up, your dog will automatically run to his bed, lie down, and be quiet. Seems almost too easy to believe, doesn't it?

Virtually every problem behavior, dog or human, can be resolved by using the power of habit. It's simply a matter of tweaking our everyday behaviors and pointing them in the right direction. Habit training is the fastest, easiest, and most stress-free way to get what you want. It's much like traveling first class on a jet compared to riding a bus.

A Note About Reliability

🦴 There are no studies that specifically delineate how long it takes or how many repetitions of an action are needed to form a habit. That being said, many behavioral scientists suggest that most habits can form in about twenty-eight days. However, once a habit is formed, that doesn't mean a dog will always be reliable with that habit. Repetition, consistency, and generalization are necessary. See Contextual Behaviors, page 13.

🦴 For puppies, a habit will not become reliable until they reach emotional maturity, which is between the ages of one and a half and three years of age.

Chapter 2

All about Habits

A habit is simply a behavior pattern or automatic routine of behaviors that is acquired by frequent repetition. A dog who jumps on people when they come in the door is often doing so out of habit. On the other hand, as I explained in Chapter 1, a dog can be trained to automatically sit whenever someone comes in the door, which is a much more appropriate habit to form. We often define habits as good or bad, although some, like putting your shoes on, are innocuous. The "good" or "bad" label depends on whether the behavior is viewed as promoting safety and health or whether it has a potential of being unsafe or harmful to people, animals, or the environment. All that being said, habits can be used as powerful tools.

Positive (good) habits help us get what we want and negative (bad) habits attract what we don't want. Good habits like exercise, being polite, and eating nutritious food attract health, make life easier for our friends and family (including our family dogs), and allow us to spend more time on other interests. Bad habits such as smoking, drinking, over-eating, or gambling outweigh healthy behavioral choices and keep us from what we really want. So depending on the habits we form, they can be used to thwart and sabotage our efforts or they can carry us toward our goals. And that includes whatever behavioral goal we've set for our dog.

> Good habits can carry us through those times we are lethargic and less motivated to want to continue.

Imagine a field of mud. If you drag a stick through the field, a rut is made. The more you drag the stick in the rut, the deeper and bigger the rut gets. If it rains, more and more water will easily flow in the rut. Your brain acts much the same way. When you perform an action repeatedly, there is specific neurological activity in the brain. Your brain "learns" this pattern of repeated behavior and a pathway is formed. In research with rats, a region in the brain called the striatum, which is related to goal-directed behavior as well as learning new habits, was active when the rats were repeatedly rewarded for running a maze. However, once running the maze became a habit, there was little activity in the striatum. The rats had "learned" how to run the maze and it had become a habit. Therefore, this goal-directed brain region was no longer activated as the rats were now running the maze on a sort of automatic pilot. A new neurological pathway had been formed and basically became a path of least resistance.

When an acquired behavior is repeated enough times it is so ingrained that it becomes involuntary and is done without conscious thought. Once we have an ingrained behavior or established routine, the brain is able to process it much more efficiently as opposed to a new task.

Actually, it's pretty easy to create new neurological pathways. Most behavioral scientists agree that, with daily repetitions, you can install a new habit in as little as twenty-eight days. Of course, the amount of time and the number of repetitions required depend on the specific situation. For example, if you move into a new house, it might take you some time to remember that the light switch in the bedroom is to the left of the door instead of to the right. But eventually you will automatically reach for the switch on the left whenever you enter the room. In my thirty-five years of dog training, I've seen new habits instilled within about twenty-eight days over and over again. However, there is a caveat to this twenty-eight-day parameter— you must consistently repeat the new behavior to establish it as a habit. Also, if you have an old habit lurking around that competes with the new one, it will generally take longer.

As easy as it is to form a new habit, it is sometimes extremely difficult to dislodge an old one. Once a pathway is formed, the "water" still wants to flow in the previous rut. If the pathway is really "deep" due to repeated actions, bad habits become addictions. The trick is to create new brain pathways rather than try to damn up the old ones. In dog training we often say, "correct the behavior, don't correct the dog." This means your goal is to create an environment where new behaviors can be formed rather than putting your dog in situations where the old behavior will be triggered and repeated. Once the new brain pathway has been created, the dog can gradually be introduced to old environments without the old habit being triggered because she now has a new, healthier pathway and behavior to choose.

How Habit Training Works

Think about how habits influence our lives and help us do what we want and get what we want. Riding a bike is a habit. Playing an instrument involves all kinds of habitual behaviors. Driving a car has many habitual components too. For example, we automatically move the steering wheel to keep us between the center lines, use the turn signal when we go around the corner (hopefully), brake when we come to a red light (again, hopefully), and pull over whenever we see an ambulance (except in some large cities, where you're on your own!). While we are doing all those things automatically, we may be mentally going over our grocery list, or thinking about the report the boss wants by tomorrow, or changing channels on the radio, or talking on the phone, or adjusting the rearview mirror. The car-driving habit that we formed gets us to where we want to go and has allowed us to become accomplished multitaskers. The down side of multitasking is that we sometimes form the bad habit of doing too many things at once and we lose our focus. An example is the rise in auto accidents that's attributed to talking on the cell phone. Once set in motion, both good and bad habits become powerhouses that affect everything we do. We can easily relate this to dog behavior. Having your dog form a habit of lying down whenever the door opens or sitting whenever he comes to a curb are two examples that have practical applications for safety.

Even the most established habits sometimes seem to disappear in the face of distractions and new situations. Have you ever forgotten your own phone number when somebody asks for it? Or maybe forgotten to put the milk back in the refrigerator after using it even though you've done it thousands of times before? This all has to do with something called contextual learning.

Contextual Behaviors

Context learning means that whenever a situation changes, to your puppy or dog, it's as if the behavior was never taught. You have to start over and teach the behavior again, from the beginning. It's as if it never existed. Here's a human example: Imagine meeting someone for the first time at a library and having a good conversation with him. Then, two weeks later, that same person greets you in the supermarket. He is dressed differently and now has a couple of children in tow. You might have a hard time remembering him because you knew him only in the context of the library, not the new context of the supermarket. But if you meet him a few more times, perhaps in several different places and situations, you will easily remember him in future meetings, no matter where they occur. This is called generalization.

Here's another example: whenever you get in your car, you buckle your seatbelt. Soon it becomes automatic and you don't have to think about it. However, when you get in the back seat of someone else's car, you might have to consciously think about buckling the seatbelt because it's a new and unusual environment. Repeat that a few times, however, and you'll automatically buckle up whenever you get in anyone's back seat.

Dogs learn the same way. For example, a dog might have learned to sit on the tiled floor in the kitchen. Then you take her into the living room and she seems to have totally forgotten what the word "sit" means. That's because the living room carpet is a different substrate and you never taught her on carpet. Similarly, asking her to sit when you've changed cologne, put a hat on, asked somebody to train with you, and so on are all separate contexts or situations. With each one you have to start over. Eventually your dog will "generalize" and, in essence, say, "I got it. You want me to sit wherever and whenever, even if the situation is new." When forming a habit, you begin to repeat a particular behavior first in one context or situation and then gradually "generalize" it by repeating it in different contexts or situations.

Children and dogs are very perceptive when it comes to contextual behavior. It only takes a child a couple of visits to the supermarket or restaurant to realize that parents treat them differently in those settings. In effect, the child says to himself, "Oh, I get it . . . when people stop and talk to you, you're not going to force me to behave. Cool, I'll yell and scream and jump on this guy instead." (Now, please realize,

14

I'm talking about *most people's children here,* not yours, of course. . . .) It's the same when you're walking your dog and people stop to chat with you; you don't pay as much attention to what your dog is doing as you usually do. Whereas the dog or the child might be addressed in no uncertain terms when it comes to unwanted behaviors at home, all of a sudden the person resorts to bribery, unenforced threats, and anything else he can think of to keep the peace. This is why it's so important to be consistent no matter where you are.

Emotions Affect Learning

Going back to the seatbelt analogy, how hard was it to learn to buckle it whenever you got in your car and make it a habit? You just did it every time you got in the car and a few weeks later, voilà, the habit of buckling your seatbelt was formed. Griping and complaining wouldn't have made learning to buckle your seatbelt any easier. How hard is it to teach a dog to sit? It's really easy but people often complain and gripe because the dog didn't sit quickly enough when asked.

The dog picks up on any and all emotional reactions on your part, even if you think you're not "being emotional." This is true whether your emotional response is resentment, frustration, anxiety, or anger—or, on the other side of the equation, happiness, joy, and love. These emotions—whether positive or negative in nature—affect the whole training process and how quickly any behavior is learned.

An important aspect of this is understanding how the context can either strengthen or weaken habitual behavior. A dog will find it much more difficult to learn something if the teacher is angry, frustrated, or impatient. The dog will much more quickly learn something if the person is having fun, encouraging, and patient. When a contextual change tempts you to discontinue your routine, thus weakening the habit, it's time to turn on your willpower switch. If that's the case, I've got you covered with entire chapters on motivation and willpower (see Chapters 9 and 10).

Successive Approximations

The trick to forming any habit is to start with baby steps, which then lead to taking bigger steps, which then eventually leads to the final goal. In psychology, these steps are referred to as successive approximations. A great example is reading this book. It's the first step (a successive approximation) in changing your behavior so you can form healthier habits which will, in turn, change your dog's habits. You're already on the road toward your goal. Way to go!

We've all heard stories of people who hadn't exercised in years and then decided to get off the couch and get going. Obviously there are many factors that influence our successes in life. I recently received an e-mail from a friend who is planning to run a marathon to raise money for a charity. Generally speaking, for the average person whose lifestyle is more or less sedentary, running a marathon may seem out of reach. How will she accomplish this herculean task? Baby steps. Depending on her current level of fitness, she'll start with small goals. Perhaps the first goal will simply be to walk ten blocks every day. Then, bit by bit, she'll progress to bigger and bigger goals by running a mile, then two miles, and so on. These progressions are successive approximations. Successive approximations are used to shape behavior. The word "shape" is the key; it means to incrementally materialize or manifest a final goal by using small pieces of the goal as goals in and of themselves. Every sentence you read in this book means you're closer to your goal of learning habit training.

Confused? Read on.

Chicken Camps

Many dog trainers attend chicken training camps to hone their "shaping" skills. The fact is if you can train a simple-minded chicken to do a complex behavior, you can use the same shaping methods to train a dog to do something.

Each trainer at my first chicken camp was given a chicken to train. For the final competition, I trained my chicken to run up a ramp, ring a bell, and then take a bow. The Japanese trainers who were attending the same camp were really creative. They used origami, the ancient art of folding paper into intricate designs, to build wrestling rings, complete with origami sumo wrestlers inside the ring. At the sound of "Hai" their chicken jumped into the origami ring and knocked over the origami wrestlers. Then the chicken jumped high in the air and rang a bell to signify his victory. And to top it all off, their chicken then spread his wings and strutted around the ring, crowing and then bowing three times. (Obviously it was a rooster.) No one could top that; the Japanese won the competition.

To teach a chicken to do complex behaviors—a series of behaviors put together to form a routine—you start by first teaching the chicken to do something simple, like touch a stick, and progress from there. Here is a general format on how this might go:

How to Train a Chicken

1. Attach a piece of food to a stick and then push it into the cage. As soon as the chicken grabs the food, "mark" the behavior with a sound. (In this book, you'll learn to "mark" behaviors with praise; in the chicken training camp we used training clickers, which are small plastic toys that make a sound similar to a cricket. I teach clicker training in my other books and in my DVDs, which you can find on my website at *www.DogWhispererDVD.com*. In this book we're concentrating on using praise as a marker so I don't teach clicker training here.)

2. The next step is to put the stick into the cage without the food and click again when the chicken touches the stick. Then reward the chicken with the food.

3. The next step is to lower the stick so the chicken has to lower his head to touch the stick. Then click and reward the chicken for lowering his head.

4. Then you remove the stick and simply watch for the chicken to lower his head. As soon as he does so, click that behavior and then reward.

5. Then you can shape the behavior even more by only clicking and rewarding the chicken if he lowers his head AND moves his foot forward.

6. Finally, if desired, you can shape the behavior even more by increasing the time the chicken has to hold that position before being rewarded.

Voilà, you now have a chicken who takes a bow. Each step was a "successive approximation" or a goal in itself that is rewarded. Then that step is used to get closer to the final goal.

Interestingly, once a chicken at the camp learned a behavior, even a routine of behaviors, he would repeat the behavior for months afterward without being asked or rewarded. It was common to see chickens on the farm jumping and twirling and bowing as part of their daily activities. I also appreciated the fact that a deal was made with the chickens that they'd never be killed for eating and that they'd spend their years on a free range being taken care of.

You've probably guessed by now how chicken training applies to what we're talking about in this book: forming habits to train dogs is accomplished by first shaping your own behavior, and then shaping your dog's behavior.

Successive approximations are small steps that are used to shape a desired behavior. Repetitions of the behavior forms a habit which leads to achieving a goal.

Cold Turkey

There is an exception to the use of successive approximations and that's the well-known process of going "cold turkey." For example, in one split second, a person might decide to say "That's it" and make a change. This happens all the time with people who have a heart attack and then follow the doctor's advice. They immediately start an exercise regimen and make changes in their diet. The motivation is so strong that the new behaviors are immediately instituted.

There's a similar principle in the dog training world called one trial conditioning. Imagine a child stepping on a puppy's tail. After that experience, there's a good chance that the puppy will stay away from the child in the future because of fear of being scared or hurt.

Realistic Expectations

I once asked my brother which he would rather have—a million dollars or peace of mind. He quickly replied, "I could buy a lot of peace of mind with a million dollars." Why not have both? The obvious caveat to that, of course, is that many of us don't want to connect our happiness and inner peace, or lack thereof, to outside influences. That's why it's called inner peace. But I digress.

Setting goals is great. There is a little matter, however, of dreaming big dreams and having realistic expectations of fulfillment. Winning the lottery, losing a bunch of weight, running a marathon, or expecting your dog to stay by your side when a squirrel runs by may seem a tad out of reach. Who's to say, for example, that my brother won't have his million dollars in the next minute. A trillion dollars? Eh, maybe not as realistic.

Expecting an eight-week-old puppy to perform complex behaviors like opening the refrigerator, getting you a soda, and then throwing the can away after you've finished it is not realistic. How about a sixteen-week-old puppy? It's in the realm of possibilities. The key is to take a step back and look at the big picture. What's realistic depends on a number of factors that pertain to *both* you and your puppy or dog:

Behavioral Influences
- Health
- Motivation
- Physical, mental, and emotional capabilities
- Temperament
- Skill levels
- Behavioral history
- Daily lifestyle
- Weather
- Distractions in the immediate environment (including the distraction of family members who are not interested in what you're trying to do)
- And a host of unknowns that might crop up

As you'll see, this book helps bring a little clarity to what's possible and what's realistically doable. The secret is, with a pinch of belief, a little know-how, and a bit of "let's just see what happens"—*it's almost **ALL** doable.*

Chapter 3

Setting Your Dog and Yourself Up for Success

"Properly trained, a man can be dog's best friend."

—Corey Ford, American writer

Common sense dictates that anything you try to do is much more likely to succeed if you do a little preparation first. In other words, set up the environment for success. If you're a builder, bring all your tools; if you're a cook, make sure all the ingredients are ready; if you're an athlete about to run a race, make sure you had a good breakfast, remembered your track shoes, and warm-up with stretching exercises before getting into the starting blocks. Being well prepared is the foundation we stand on.

The same holds true for raising and training your dog. Preparation is the key. This brings us to the Nine Ingredients for Optimum Health and Growth, which I write about extensively in both *The Dog Whisperer* and *The Puppy Whisperer* books.

23

The Nine Ingredients

There are many influences in life that affect both our dog's and our own behavior. We need a rock-solid foundation that supports us and makes everything we do easier to do, including forming healthier new habits.

The Nine Ingredients are:

1. Food (a high-quality diet)
2. Play
3. Socialization
4. Quiet Time (relaxation)
5. Exercise
6. Employment (mental stimulation)
7. Rest (proper sleep)
8. Education (training and discipline)
9. Health Care (including dental health)

If these crucial ingredients are provided in a balanced manner, they are stepping stones to a healthy body and a healthy life and support all of our thoughts and actions in a positive way. But if a sufficient quantity or quality of each ingredient is not provided, a roadblock occurs and physical, mental, and emotional health is compromised. As a result, all behavior, as well as our motivation and willpower to do anything, suffers.

It isn't necessary to be perfect. Frankly, it's unlikely that it's even possible to be perfect. We all have busy lives and a myriad of commitments. And, after all, we can still thrive even if we don't get the same amount of food or sleep or fun

Figure 3-1

The Nine Ingredients for Optimum Health and Growth

time each day. The same is true for our dogs. The trick is integrating all of these life requirements as part of our lives on a fairly consistent basis—in other words, making all of these good habits. Balance is the goal and consistency the key.

Let's look at an example of the ways in which an imbalance of just a few of the Nine Ingredients can affect your dog's behavior. Maybe you decide to teach your dog a fun trick like "playing the piano" to show off to your friends. Even small dogs can be taught to jump on the piano bench so they can reach the keys and then hit them. But if either you or your dog is distracted and unable to concentrate due to hunger pangs, pain, and/or lethargy caused by a diet that's deficient in high-quality nutrients, a lack of sleep, a lack of proper exercise, or an aching tooth, it will be really tough for you to teach the trick or for your dog to learn it. The more alert you are, the better. Providing the proper balance of the Nine Ingredients can really affect the success of your training—and even impact your safety and your dog's safety.

Whenever you have a problem with your dog or with yourself, review the list of Nine Ingredients. If any ingredient seems to be a roadblock because it is deficient in quantity or quality, use the formula of habit training to bring it into balance. (See page 57.)

Ingredient #1: Food (a high-quality diet)
   🦴   Keep away from foods containing sugars, by-products, artificial colors, and additives. Many canine nutritionists also suggest limiting the amount of

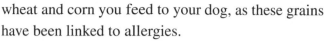

wheat and corn you feed to your dog, as these grains have been linked to allergies.

☙ Use a dog food made of high-grade ingredients, preferably with organic, free-range meat. Many holistic veterinarians are now recommending a raw meat diet. Read up on raw meat and its benefits.

☙ Never give your dog chocolate, grapes, raisins, onions, greasy foods, or cooked bones. Chocolate, grapes, raisins, and onions can be harmful to some (though not all) dogs. Too many greasy foods can cause pancreatitis. Never feed your dog any bones from meat that's been cooked because it can splinter or cause choking. Also, make sure your dog or puppy can't get into the trash bin to retrieve any forbidden foods. (Note: Raw poultry bones do not splinter like cooked ones and are therefore not as dangerous.)

☙ Add fresh fruits, like apples and watermelon, and vegetables, like carrots and zucchini, to your dog's diet.

☙ Whenever changing your dog's diet, do so gradually to give her a chance to acclimate to the new food.

Ingredient #2: Play

☙ Engage in a variety of games, including include Fetch with tennis balls and Frisbees, Tug, Find It, Hide-and-go-seek (Peek-a-boo, see page 98), and running obstacle courses with tunnels, steps and jumps.

The Nine Ingredients for Optimum Health and Growth

Ingredient	Qualities	Short-Term Benefits
1. Food	Feeling good physically and mentally	Full of energy
2. Play	Feeling good physically and mentally	Relieves stress; improves mental and physical health; raises stress management threshold
3. Socialization	Opportunity to learn proper dog etiquette; greater safety with people and other animals; builds confidence	Teaches safety through appropriate behavior; improves physical and mental health
4. Quiet Time	Relaxation	Calm, relaxed behavior
5. Exercise	Relieves stress; promotes mental and physical health	Relieves stress; improves mental and physical health; raises stress management threshold
6. Employment (mental stimulation)	Feeling good physically and mentally; redirects energy from destructive behavior to appropriate behavior	Relieves stress; improves mental and physical health; raises stress management threshold
7. Rest (proper sleep)	Relaxation	Relieves stress; improves mental and physical health
8. Education (training and discipline)	Feeling good physically and mentally	Safety; teaches appropriate behaviors; good human-dog relationship
9. Health Care (including dental health, good hygiene, and grooming care)	Feeling good physically and mentally	Maintains mental and physical health

Long-Term Benefits	Signs of a Roadblock (too little or too much)
Long, healthy life	Hunger; lethargy; overweight or too thin
Teaches safety through appropriate behavior; improves physical and mental health; forms a trusting bond between dog and human	Chewing and other behavioral problems; poor health; aggression
Teaches safety through appropriate behavior; improves physical and mental health	Chewing and other behavioral problems; poor health; aggression
Good health; calm dog	Anxious; mouthy, chewy, and other behavioral problems
Improves physical and mental health	Chewing and other behavioral problems; poor health; aggression
Improves physical and mental health; appropriate behaviors become habits	Chewing, digging, stealing, and other behavioral problems, poor health; aggression
Improves physical and mental health	Chewing, digging, stealing and other behavioral problems; poor health; aggression
Improves physical and mental health; appropriate behaviors become habits	Chewing, digging, stealing, and other behavioral problems; poor health; aggression; jumping on people
Maintains mental and physical health	Sickness, short life, lethargy, aggression

Ingredient #3: Socialization

🦴 Take your dog with you whenever possible, including to work and when running errands. Note: Remember that your dog could suffer from heatstroke if she's left in a car or yard in hot weather. Cracking a car window for some fresh air doesn't help in hot weather when the temperature inside rises as the sun bakes down on it. And remember, too, that a car that's parked in the shade one minute can be in full sun the next as the sun moves. If the temperature is 85 degrees Fahrenheit outside on a hot summer day, the inside of the car can reach 120 degrees Fahrenheit within half an hour. Your dog can suffer brain damage or death if her body temperature reaches 107 degrees Fahrenheit, which is only 5 to 7 degrees above normal body temperature. (A dog's normal temperature ranges between 100 and 102.5 degrees Fahrenheit.)

🦴 Attend dog training classes including, if possible, classes in agility, water work, service training, and tracking.

Ingredient #4: Quiet Time (relaxation)

🦴 Teach your dog to go to his own spot and teach people, especially children, to leave the dog alone when he's resting.

Ingredient #5: Exercise

🦴 Incorporate daily exercise: Ask your vet about the types and amount of exercise that's right for your dog, including aerobic (running and walking), strength (pulling and uphill treks), balance (walking bleacher steps, doing agility, and teaching "beg" (smaller dogs only). Be careful about overexertion on hot days and be sure your dog has sufficient water. On a long walk or hike, be sure to take water along for your dog.

🦴 Massage your dog frequently. It's a great bonding tool.

Ingredient #6: Employment (mental stimulation)

🦴 Give your dog a "job" to do such as teaching Find It, Fetch, and how to put toys in a toy box.

🦴 Teach your dog to dig in "approved," specific areas of the yard only.

🦴 Use automated toys such as automatic tennis ball machines and treat-dispensing toys such as the Kong dispenser, which automatically dispenses a "fresh" Kong on a timed schedule.

Ingredient #7: Rest (proper sleep)

🦴 Set a schedule or routine where your dog can sleep without being interrupted.

🦴 Unless you are really certain that your dog won't bite, tell children never to wake him with touch. Instead use sounds like light clapping or whistling to awaken him and be careful that you don't scare him awake. And be especially cautious when waking a dog who is whining or moving or "running" in his sleep.

Ingredient #8: Education (training and discipline)

- Teach the basic behaviors of sit, down, stay, come, go-to-spot, find it, leave it, drop it, and walk without pulling.
- Get your dog used to noise, motion, and touch.

Ingredient #9: Health Care

- See your vet on a regular basis.
- Include dental care in your dog's hygiene routine and get his teeth cleaned when needed.
- Grooming contributes to hygiene and health. Some dogs need much more grooming care than others. Set up a grooming schedule based on your dog's specific needs, which are dictated by his breed's coat type.

By keeping the Nine Ingredients in balance, you are providing a rock-solid foundation and the healthiest environment possible for success.

Creating a Safe Environment That Promotes Success

Positive training is rooted in love, compassion, safety, and fun. Controlling your dog's freedom goes a long way toward shaping positive behavior and forming good habits. It's the same premise that you would use with a child. You would never give a child a box of crayons and say, "Honey, I'm leaving for the day. Don't use these crayons." Or, if someone has a bad habit of overeating, you wouldn't expect much success if that person holds business meetings at the local pancake house for breakfast, lunch, and dinner. Similarly, you can't:

- 🦴 Put a dog who has a habit of digging in a yard and say, "Don't dig" OR
- 🦴 Put a dog who has a habit of chewing in a room full of slippers and say, "Don't chew" OR
- 🦴 Put a dog who has a habit of jumping in a room full of family members and say, "Don't jump" OR
- 🦴 Give a dog who has a habit of barking at the mail carrier free access to the front window and say, "Don't bark."

A successful environment is one where a dog *can't* do anything you don't want her to do. Left on her own, a dog's errant behavior can quickly become a "bad" habit because it becomes self-reinforced. In other words, the digging, chewing, jumping, and barking habits continue because they are all mentally and physically stimulating. These behaviors feel good because they often relieve boredom, pent-up energy, and stress. So it's important to set up the environment so the behaviors can't happen. It's all about discipline and that means it's our responsibility to set rules and create behavioral boundaries.

In a nutshell, a disciplined environment is similar to "home-schooling" a child. Our role as educators and as our dog's "life coach" is to first-and-foremost create an environment that optimizes learning. Leadership simply means controlling everything your dog wants and using positive, nonviolent methods to teach him that he gets whatever he wants as long as he behaves appropriately.

The key to making this happen is setting up an environment that keeps you, your dog, and the environment safe.

Once this environment is set up, we can teach our dogs what to do step-by-step and also what not to do. As a result, they learn self-control. They learn that their behavior gets them what they want. This fosters a confident, calm personality. In addition, a safe environment allows dogs to experience the world on their own. They learn to survive their mistakes and gain confidence from their successes. This leads to a topic that I stress over and over again—safety through prevention and management.

Restraining and Confining

Parents are experts at preventing problems by setting up safe environments for their children. To keep a child safe, the parent baby-proofs the environment by picking things up off the floor, removing breakable items from the coffee table and end tables, putting safety latches on the cupboards, and so on. The parent also confines the child in specific areas by using baby gates and playpens. And the parent holds the child's hand whenever necessary, such as when climbing steps and crossing streets. It's exactly the same with a dog. Until the dog is reliable, it's necessary to "dog-proof" the environment and to also keep the dog under physical control. Sounds logical, doesn't it? The problem is, restricting a dog's freedom goes against human nature. For one thing, not being able to do what we want, when we want, doesn't feel safe. In addition, fear and frustration are easily triggered if our actions are, in essence, handcuffed by someone else. So seeing a dog tied up often elicits our sympathy. We're "softies" at heart.

Both dogs and humans have an aversion to being restrained and confined. *Restraining* means freedom is restricted by being tethered; *confining* means freedom is restricted within boundaries such as being behind a barrier such as a baby gate, door, exercise pen, or fence.

Part of the enjoyment of living with a dog is the fact that we live vicariously through them. Dogs remind us of our sense of inner freedom and natural state of living in the moment. Seeing a dog run free and play and jump strikes a primal cord of joy within all of us. So what's the answer? The trick is to not only change the way your dog feels about being restrained and confined, but also how you feel about restricting your dog's freedom. This is done by counter-conditioning. Counter-conditioning is a process where you change the way you or your dog feels about something by substituting an opposite reaction.

For example, tethering a dog to something feels crummy to some people because it's taking away her freedom. But when you think about it, walking your dog on a leash is actually a form of tethering. So changing the way you *think* about it changes the way you *feel* about it. What if you taught your dog to bring you her leash so you can both go for a walk? This trick is fun and enjoyable. So by associating this trick with walking, you've changed the way you feel about tethering. You've actually counter-conditioned the way you feel about restraining your dog *and* you've changed the way your dog feels about being restrained.

Here's another example: forcing a dog into a crate feels crummy to you and your dog too. But imagine teaching your dog to voluntarily run into his "office" and pull the door closed behind him! What a great trick! By associating the kennel with the word "office" you've changed the way you feel about it and made the exercise a fun thing to do. In addition, by associating the kennel with play, dinner time, and great treats, dogs can learn to absolutely *love* the idea of going into a kennel. So, if you like this idea, instead of saying "kennel" or "crate," you will forevermore use the word "office" when you want your dog to go there.

By simply shifting your perception and looking at the kennel in a playful way, dogs and people feel an immediate difference. Rather than looking at restraining and confining as something dreadful, the training process now becomes a game. It becomes fun. Here are a couple of perception shifters that help elucidate the technique of counter-conditioning:

- If a child falls and gets a boo-boo, rather than offering to kiss it and make it better, teach the child to take a bow and say "Ta Da!"
- Rather than coddle your dog when you accidently step on his tail say, "Yay! That was exciting! Here's a piece of chicken!"

Collars and Harnesses

Positive training employs the use of collars and harnesses that will not in any way inflict pain. We do not use *choke collars*, also referred to as *training collars* or *slip collars*, prong collars, or shock collars, all of which are unacceptable because of the potential for hurting the dog. The use of these types of collar is based on the premise that you need to inflict pain or discomfort to get your dog to do what you want. The bottom line is that it is not necessary to use any jerking at all to get your dog to do what you want.

Here are the collars and harnesses that I recommend:

For puppies and smaller dogs: Choose a body harness collar that fits around the front half of the body.

For medium to large dogs: Choose a Martingale-style collar, such as the one from Premier Pet Products. Martingale collars don't close completely around the dog's neck and therefore eliminate the potential for a choking problem.

For dogs who pull on the leash:

- First, try a body harness, like the Easy Walker by Premier Pet Products or the Halti Harness, designed by Dr. Roger Mugford. These harnesses are designed to inhibit pulling.
- Head-halter-style collars (also called nose harness collars) are also good for dogs who pull. There are several brands and styles that I recommend including the Gentle Leader from Premier; the Halti Headcollar designed by Dr. Roger Mugford; and K9 Bridle, which is made in England. They work on the premise that where the head goes, the body follows. Most dogs adjust easily to these collars. However, be sure to give the dog enough slack to greet another dog,

which sometimes involves looking away, sniffing the ground, or turning his side to the other dog.

Some people mistake halter-type collars for muzzles and therefore think that dogs who are wearing this type of collar are dangerous. However, unlike muzzles, dogs can bark, eat, and drink, and even bite with halter-style collars on. To offset this concern, I suggest choosing a collar that blends with the color of the dog's coat or a brightly colored one that makes people think the collar is fun and nonthreatening.

Whatever collar or harness you select, be sure it's not too tight. You should be able to place two fingers between the collar and the dog's neck. (See Figure 3-2)

Figure 3-2

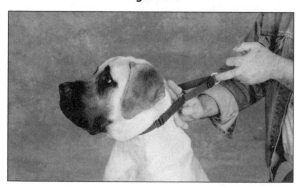

Premier's Martingale-style collar

Figure 3-3

Gentle Leader halter-style collar

Figure 3-4

Easy Walk anti-pulling harness
attached to a bungee leash

Proper Use of Leashes and Tethers

Unless you use the proper methods to put a leash on a dog for the first time, he will hate it. He'll pull and squirm and chew and do everything he can to try to escape. So why do most dogs get excited whenever someone reaches for a leash? What happened to change the way the dog feels about the leash? Over time, the dog came to associate the leash with something he loves, going for a walk. This process of changing the way a dog feels about something he dislikes to something he likes is another example of counter-conditioning. If your puppy or dog chews the tether or leash, use a chew-proof tether such as the one available at *www.DogWhispererDVD.com*.

Acclimating a Puppy or Dog to a Leash or Tether

If your new dog is a puppy or one of the small percentage of dogs who hasn't been acclimated to a leash, follow these steps to get him used to being restrained and help him form a positive association to being tethered.

1. Attach a very lightweight leash to the collar just before you put his dinner dish down. Then remove it after he finishes eating. Repeat for every meal for a few days.
2. Progress to leaving the leash on after he finishes eating for longer and longer periods of time and let him drag it around while you play with him.
3. Finally, progress to picking up the leash and holding it while he eats. Step by step you'll gradually get him used to being tethered so he actually enjoys it.

Tethering Procedure

1. Attach the tether to a sturdy chair or table leg, an eye hook on a baseboard, or position the tether under a closed door as pictured in Figure 3-5. Hook the tether to your dog's Martingale or buckle collar. You can also use a body harness but since little pressure is being exerted on your dog's neck, a regular collar is acceptable. Do not use a choke collar. Until he learns to associate "good things" with being tethered, it's normal for a dog to use a low level of resistance and occasional pulling in response to being restrained. The trick to getting your dog to actually enjoy being tethered is to go at a rate that he can handle without any distress.

Figure 3-5   **Figure 3-6**

Figure 3-7

The safest way to tether your dog to a door: Slip the leash handle over the doorknob on the other side of the door, drop the leash to the floor, and slip it under the door. Then close the door. Never tether your dog unless you are there to supervise.

2. To redirect your dog's attention and take his mind off being restrained, you can get down on the floor, make "kissy" sounds, and distract him by playing the Find It game, which is taught in Chapter 7. Be careful to throw the treat within the range that he can reach. Repeat this five to ten times.

3. Next, kneel directly in front of your dog, no more than twelve inches away. Hold a food treat in one hand, close both hands, and place them in starting position on your chest. (Note: Dogs are distracted by any type of movement, so this "hands-on-chest" starting position is helpful in training most behaviors.) Now ask your dog to sit

and then give the hand signal for "sit" by placing the treat slightly over his head. When he sits, praise lavishly and give him the treat. To get him up from the sit, say "find it" and throw a treat off to the side. Then ask him to sit again. Repeat this sequence five to ten times.

4. Next, get up and stand directly in front of your dog, still no more than twelve inches away. Repeat the previous sequence from the standing position.

5. Next, still with your hands in starting position on your chest holding a treat, look at your dog and, without doing anything else, wait for him to sit. Do not say the word "sit" or give him the hand signal. He may pull, move side to side, jump, and move in circles. While he is doing all these things, he'll probably feel an occasional gentle pressure from the restraining tether. If so, take his mind off it by making distracting "kissy" sounds. Wait up to forty-five seconds for him to sit. He should sit without being asked. When he does, praise lavishly, pet him and give him a jackpot of many treats. If he doesn't sit, go back to step 3 and repeat it until he is successful; then return to steps 4 and 5.

6. Now get him up so you can repeat the process by saying "Find it" and throwing a treat off to the side, within his range. Now, once again, remain standing in the same position with your hands on your chest and say nothing while you wait for him to sit. Your dog will sit and you will again reward effusively with petting, praise, and treats. Repeat this sequence until your dog will sit within three seconds. Here's what's going on—the

length of time between giving a dog a signal and the dog doing the behavior is called latency. When the dog does a behavior within a 0 to 3 second latency, it means that he understands what you are asking of him in that particular situation.

Each time you start the sequence, it will take him some time to actually sit because of the newness of the game and the distraction of the tether. Once he figures it out, which is normally within ten sequences, he will sit faster and faster. When he sits within three seconds, back up another foot, so you are now two feet from him.

Starting from two feet away, begin the whole process again. Gradually increase your distance a foot at time until you are 20 feet away. This is done over a period of time. Do only 5 to 10 repetitions in each session. End each session while your dog is still enjoying it. As a matter of fact, you should end any session at any point you feel your dog is getting distressed. A small amount of stress is okay, distressed is not.

Progress is signaled when your dog will sit within three seconds at each distance and will do so three times in a row. So the sequence would look like this:

🦴 Start at twelve inches. Dog sits, praise, pet, and give a treat. Find it. Repeat. When dog sits within three seconds from the start of the sequence and does

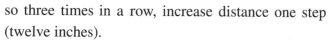

so three times in a row, increase distance one step (twelve inches).

- From a distance of two feet, wait for your dog to sit. When he does, approach, praise, pet, and treat. When he sits within three seconds from the start of the sequence and does so three times in a row, increase the distance another foot—to about three feet.

- Repeat this routine. Each time your dog has been successful three times in a row, add another step of distance.

With the knowledge that dogs hate to be restrained, it would be pure abuse to tie a dog to something and let him exhaust himself trying to get free. The process must be positive and it must be done in baby steps.

If done correctly, which means step-by-step, the dog is not traumatized in the least. As a matter of fact, within a few sessions, a dog can learn to love to be tethered because he has only positive associations with it.

Improper tethering can lead to strangulation or other injuries so never tether a dog unless that dog is supervised.

When to Tether—the 75 Percent Rule

Until you feel safe that your dog will leave your cushions, slippers, table legs, and other chewables alone and won't sneak away to leave puddles or piles, it's recommended that when you're home you keep her tethered close to you up to 75 percent of her "awake" time. This might seem like a lot, but most dogs are awake only six to eight hours a day. Remember, even when tethering is done according to guidelines, safety concerns still exist. Therefore, your dog should be tethered only when you are in the same room and able to supervise.

As your dog becomes more reliable, you can reduce the amount of time she is tethered. The more reliable she is, the more freedom she gets.

By tethering and crating or kenneling your dog, you avoid ever having to use physical punishment. Bad habits such as begging at the table, jumping, stealing, and bolting out the door don't exist because the dog isn't able to do any of these things. The good habits you want to teach your dog are easily formed because those desirable behaviors, such as chewing on appropriate toys, sitting when people enter the room, lying down on her bed when you're eating dinner, jumping only when invited, and so on are the only ones that are rewarded and reinforced. Your dog will become more and more reliable and able to be around you and visitors without any concerns about inappropriate behavior. Eventually you won't have to even think of the behavior problems because they will simply fade away.

How to Use Tethering to Eliminate Problem Behaviors

If Your Dog...

Jumps	Tether her and then...	Teach her to sit or lie down instead
Chews	Tether her and then...	Teach her to play Tug and chew appropriate objects or grab a toy instead
Gets on furniture that you don't want her on	Tether her and then...	Teach her to lie at your feet or go to her bed instead
Eliminates in the house	Tether her and then...	Teach her to eliminate outside instead

Kennel Training

The kennel is a very helpful management tool. Even if you don't plan to use it all the time, it can be important in case you need to kennel your puppy or dog for travel or if he's hospitalized at the vet's. If your dog or puppy is already happy and confident about being in a kennel, you can skip this section. If not, read on. Your goal is to get your dog accustomed to chew on toys, rest, and sleep while confined in the kennel. And the kennel can also be a tremendous help in housetraining.

A puppy or dog who is not used to the kennel should be acclimated to it slowly, gradually increasing the time spent in it by very small increments. Watch for signs of distress, like excessive barking, drooling, pacing, or trying to chew through the bars. If your puppy or dog exhibits any of these signs go back as many steps in the process as you need to in order to make her comfortable again.

Do not kennel a dog who cries or whines for longer than twenty minutes or tries to escape by chewing on the bars of the kennel. If you follow the incremental steps I'm sharing here, this type of behavior shouldn't occur. If it does, your dog is exhibiting separation anxiety and needs the attention of a qualified trainer or behaviorist. Continued kenneling will likely result in serious injury and/or more severe behavioral problems.

Kennel Training Tips

🦴 Feed your dog's meals in the kennel, with the door open. As soon as he isn't showing any hesitation about going in his kennel for his meal, close the door until the meal is finished.

🦴 When your puppy or dog isn't looking, put some treats in the kennel. Soon he'll learn to go into it to look for them.

🦴 Whenever your dog enters the kennel on his own, immediately praise him and throw him highly valued food treats such as chicken, turkey, cheese, and so on. By doing so, you're playing the magnet game, which you'll learn in Chapter 6.

In Chapter 11, "Basic Behaviors," you'll learn how to get your dog to go to the kennel.

Chapter 4

The Motivating Power of Play

I know many dogs who would rather chase a ball than eat a piece of chicken. Just like us, play is rooted in a dog's primal bones and, oh, the good it does. Play teaches body coordination, releases endorphins that make us feel good, keeps us in shape, and relieves stress.

Kids and dogs don't need to be taught to play. It's natural. So what's up with some of us adults? Many of us seem to have lost our motivation to play and, as a result, both we and our dogs suffer the consequences. The desire to play past the age of childhood is one of the strongest similarities between humans and dogs. This chapter is all about getting up, getting motivated, and getting going again with our fun-loving dogs. Let's take advantage of our common ground. Let's get it on!

Learning Through Play

Biologists and psychologists have discovered that the young of an enormous number of animal species, including humans, gain much of their knowledge from playing. In fact, through play we and many other animals learn about the nature of the world as well as ways to stay safe and survive that are completely original. In other words, we are able to learn new and creative strategies for dealing with life by trying them out in a "playful" way.

Humans can learn by imitation or by direct instruction from an elder. But when we learn in these ways we're simply learning how to do things the same way they've been done before. In play, we can try out things in a way that is different than anyone has done before. We can enlarge our repertoire of responses to different situations that may arise in life. Evolutionary biologist Mark Bekoff calls this "training for the unexpected."

The reason that new and creative behavior arises in play is because it isn't "for keeps." In other words, we (and dogs, and many other mammals, birds, and perhaps even reptiles and insects) "know" that when we play, our behavior will not have lasting consequences that might threaten our survival. That's because we are only *pretending* to chase, or run away from, or take something from someone, so we feel safe to try out risky maneuvers. If we get caught, we won't really be in any danger. The safety and innate pleasure of play encourages creativity, learning, and behavioral change. Most scientific research on play has focused on its role in childhood development. However, an increasing amount of evidence now suggests that play can continue to be a powerful learning tool for humans and other animals in adulthood.

> Play is like practicing for life, so that you can get better at it!

Building good play habits provides an enormous opportunity for communication, improving physical and mental health, and learning mutually rewarding life lessons.

Communicating Through Play

Nature has provided your dog with impulses for fighting and hunting, which are natural and, in the wild, necessary for survival. Unfortunately, those impulses aren't really useful for life in the human home. Without a good outlet, your dog is left to channel her hunting impulses into tearing apart your sofa, chasing your shoelaces, and pouncing on the cat. The good news is that you can use play to channel those impulses into more appropriate activities.

Games like Tug teach a dog how to use his mouth appropriately, how to cooperate with you, and how self-control can be rewarding and fun. Through the game of Tug dogs learn that it is rewarding for them to share objects with you rather than compete over them, that it is inappropriate to put their mouths on you or any other human, and that biting and pulling is appropriate only on very specific toy objects. (See Tug in Chapter 7.) Many people wonder if playing games of Tug will make their dogs aggressive. The answer is, if you play Tug in the way described in this book, there is no danger of increasing your dog's aggressive behavior. In fact, the opposite is actually true.

Play is the common language that is shared between us. Through play, we let our dogs know what kind of behavior we expect from them. For example:

- Playing Peek-a-boo, a form of hide-and-go-seek, teaches him to look for you instead of chasing the kid on the skateboard.
- Playing Find It, which is a form of tracking, teaches him to focus on you rather than guard the house from the mail carrier.
- Playing Fetch teaches him to put his mouth on tennis balls and Frisbees rather than the sofa and bunny slippers.
- Teaching him to jump over a stick or run through tunnels teaches him to follow you as his leader rather than chase squirrels.
- Teaching him to play dead or rest his head on the floor helps teach him to relax.
- Teaching him to balance something on his nose teaches him to not mind being examined around the face by the vet or trimmed by the groomer.
- Teaching him to shake teaches him to not mind having his nails clipped or being handled by the veterinarian.

Figure 4-1

Teaching your dog to jump is
a form of play that reduces
stress and encourages him to
pay attention to you.

The games of Find It, Peek-a-boo, Fetch, and Tug build
confidence, coordination, and redirect your puppy or dog's
attention to you. They improve health, reduce stress and raise
his stress management threshold so he can handle life's challenges. So, even on the days when you have no time to do any
other training with your dog, take a couple of minutes and
play. Daily play will teach your dog some of his most important lessons. And patience is one of them. In the bargain, you
and he will both have fun, will reduce your stress levels, and
will strengthen the emotional bond between you.

Figure 4-2

Teaching a dog to shake is a form
of play that helps desensitize him
to having his nails clipped or being
handled by the veterinarian.

Teaching your dog to wait for a toy to be thrown, to wait
for the door to open, or to wait while you prepare his food
fosters cooperation instead of competition. He'll be more
patient at the vet's and groomer's and with a little practice,
be more accepting when small children step on a tail or poke,
prod, and pull him. Training becomes a game rather than a
battle of wills.

Respect Boundaries

Teaching behavioral boundaries to your dog is a special challenge because dogs tend to have a different idea of how much

is too much. They like to jump, bump, and pounce in fun, and have no awareness that it might be hurtful or dangerous to humans. And when dogs get excited they naturally want to use their mouths. Playtime provides an excellent opportunity to teach your dog appropriate behavioral boundaries.

Teaching boundaries to a puppy or dog is no different than teaching a child. Playing often involves a lot of physical activity, even rough physical activity. Playing teaches children to identify with the emotional and physical feelings of others. When a child gets hurt, she says, "Ow" or "Stop!" and she stops playing. Nobody wants to play with someone who causes pain and injury so children learn to stop hurting one another. Dogs play with each other in the same way. If one gets hurt, the other stops doing whatever caused the pain. Basically, dogs adhere to the same unspoken Golden Rule as people: Do unto others as you would have them do unto you. If there are physical or emotional boundaries you do not want others to cross, make them clear, then make sure you respect them yourself.

Playing games with your dog is a lot more fun when you are sure that your dog will respect your boundaries. You, of course, will also have to respect your dog's boundaries. Dogs are very honest about this kind of thing. So, if you hit them, yell at them, shake them, shock them, pinch them, etc., they will not play with you. Period.

The bottom line is that play is shaped by rules. The qualities that make play possible include patience, trust, and empathy. Within those guidelines, play is an improvisation. Just like life.

Making Life Playful

Attitude is everything. If it's fun for you, it's fun for your dog. If getting up to play with your dog seems like a chore, take a break and take a breath. Sometimes the trick is just to start again with a fresh perspective. Once you've established good habits, safe and nondestructive play becomes the norm rather than the exception.

Chapter 5

The Four Steps for Habit Power

"To everything there is a season, and a time to every purpose under the heaven."

—Ecclesiastes iii.1

Now it's time to get down to the nitty-gritty of forming new habits. It's play time. This simple program will establish and maintain good habits and make training fun.

All good habits are formed using these four Habit Power steps:

1. Identify Your Goal
2. Form a Strategy
3. Implement the Strategy
4. Maintain the New Habit

Here's how it works:

Step 1: Identify Your Goal

If we don't know what we want, we can't get it. And if we humans don't know what we want our dogs to do, how the heck can they ever figure it out? The first step to forming a good habit is to specifically identify the goal.

Be as specific as you can be. For example, if you want ice cream, say how much you want, when you want it, and the flavor you want. Otherwise you might get a teaspoon of vanilla when you really wanted a bowlful of chocolate. Here's an example in training your dog: What do you want your puppy or dog to do when people walk in the door? When I ask people that question, they usually say, "To stop jumping." Instead, the trick is to identify the behavior you *do* want instead, such as, "I want my dog to immediately sit whenever someone walks in the door." If your dog is sitting, clearly he's *not* jumping. You simply redirected him to the behavior you wanted which, in this case, is sitting.

> With positive training it's not about stopping a behavior; it's about redirecting the dog to do something else instead.

To express this principle in a different way, it's important that you always ask yourself what you want your dog TO DO and not what you want your dog to stop doing. This is the key to everything, especially training your dog. Think substitution; not suppression. If you're trying to break a bad habit, choose a behavior that is incompatible with the habit you are trying to change. When I gave up smoking, I practiced a specific breathing exercise every time I got the urge to smoke. That worked for me. Some people decide to exercise more as a "stop smoking" ploy and find that the chemical changes wrought by the exercise satisfies the urge to smoke. To use a canine example, let's say you want your dog to stop jumping or bolting when you're out on walks. To do that, you will proactively install an opposing behavior such as teaching your dog to sit or lie down whenever you come to a stop.

Step 2: Form a Strategy

After deciding on your goal, you'll need to then identify the new habits that will help you reach it. It's those habits that make up your strategy. They are the tools that will get you to your goal.

Step 3: Implement the Strategy

Like the old Nike commercial, implementing a strategy means, "Just do it." If your goal is to train your dog to automatically sit or lie down whenever you come to a stop, you'll simply follow the step-by-step strategy of consistently asking your dog to sit or lie down whenever you come to a stop until the behavior becomes a habit. Or, for another example, if your goal is to get healthy, you'll simply follow the strategy of daily exercise and improved diet habits that you've set up.

Although the number of repetitions needed to form a habit cannot be measured because of various factors such as the person's consistency, desire, and motivation, there's a ball-park time-frame of around twenty-eight days. It's safe to say you'll "soon" find yourself doing a behavior automatically. At that point it has become a habit. Repetition and consistency are the keys to forming habits.

Here are some memory triggers that can assist you in reinforcing the new habits:

- ⌘ Paste reminder notes in various places such as near the doorknob, on the bathroom mirror, on the coffee pot, etc. Memory experts tell us that, over time, we become habituated to these notes. So, to make sure they are effective, occasionally move them to new places and use different colors of paper and ink when you do so. That will help your brain to access the information on the notes.
- ⌘ Use your kitchen timer, the alarm on your watch or clock, and your cell phone to remind you to do things.
- ⌘ Put electronic reminder notes on your computer or PDA.
- ⌘ Talk about your new habits with friends and family. If it feels right with certain people, give them permission to tweak your memory with friendly reminders. There is one caveat to this tip—only discuss your new habits with friends and family who will be supportive. Don't put yourself in the position of having to argue or defend yourself.

Once a habit forms, you'll only have to consciously think about what you're doing on an occasional basis to strengthen it. Then the habit will continue of its own accord.

So what happens if you can't seem to do what you want to do? In other words, once you've started to implement your strategy you find both your motivation and willpower aren't as strong as you thought they were? The answer to that is to simply identify those as your goals. Then use these same Four Steps for Habit Power to improve and empower your motivation and willpower.

The coolest way to speed the process of making a behavior a habit is to really dig what you're doing. Use your feelings as fuel. It's all about forming an emotional attachment with the new behavior you're trying to habitualize. When I was in high school, I had a summer job in a factory that made coffee makers. My job was to twist wires together. All day long, that's what I did—twisting wires together over and over and over. It was pretty mundane and extremely boring. What kept me from going crazy was thinking about my goal. Every coffee maker I worked on got me closer to buying my own car at the end of the summer. With that goal foremost in my mind, I formed a wire-twisting habit that enabled me to make even more coffee makers, which earned me more money and enabled me to buy my very own car.

Here's a doggie example: Let's say you're trying to form a daily habit of taking your dog for a walk. This is a good habit to form, both because of the health benefits and because it actually brings you both closer together. This results in a dog who is more likely to listen to you when you ask him to do something and it helps relieve stress so your dog is much more relaxed. If the thought of taking your dog for a walk is something you're not thrilled about, think about how you'd feel about going for a walk it if your dog came up to you with a leash in his mouth. I don't know of anyone who would refuse to take their dog for a walk and not feel good about doing it if their dog is standing there with those puppy-dog eyes, holding a leash. So by simply teaching your dog to fetch his leash, that behavior will soon become a habit and your dog will automatically get his leash every day after dinner. One habit leads to another. Ta Da! (Fetching is taught in Chapter 7, Games to Play on Vacation.)

By internalizing and integrating the "feel-good" experiences with your goals and the new habits you're forming, you will also quickly create new set-points. In other words, you'll be feeling and acting differently. You will project more confidence through less body movement, which helps keep your dog focused on you instead of being distracted. You will be more concentrated, yet more relaxed. In short, you'll be more of a leader. Your dog will pick up on this because dogs respond to our energy.

Step 4: Maintain the New Habit

Once a habit is formed, you'll only have to reinforce it intermittently. For example, if your dog is now automatically sitting every time you stop at the street, you'll no longer have to use treats and praise because the behavior is solidified. It's exactly like you automatically buckling your seat belt. Every once in a while you'll have to remind yourself but for all intents and purposes, it's automatic.

Using the Four Steps for Habit Power

Here's how to use the Four Steps for Habit Power for a specific dog training goal:

Step 1: Identify Your Goal

"On walks, I want my dog to automatically stop and sit every time we get to a street corner." *It's important that you identify exactly what it is you want. If you don't have the goal firmly entrenched in your mind, it's less likely you'll be successful.*

Step 2: Form a Strategy

Identify the habit(s) to be formed that will lead to the goal:

Habit #1: Put daily walks on a schedule. 7 A.M. and 7 P.M.

Habit #2: Step on my dog's leash whenever I stop walking, at street corners and when I stop to talk to a neighbor. By doing this, you are using the tool of prevention, since your dog is unable to continue to walk or jump as long as your foot is on the leash.

Habit #3: Teach my dog to sit whenever I stop. I'll repeat this three times at every street corner before actually continuing my walk. By taking a few steps back and having your dog repeat the behavior of walking to the corner and sitting one to three times, you are using these repetitions to more quickly form the habit as well as remove your dog's anticipation of you going into the street after one stop.

Habit #4: Play the magnet game and give my dog a treat whenever he sits without being asked. The first time your dog sits within three seconds of you coming to a stop, jackpot him. This means give your dog enthusiastic praise and many treats because he has figured out what he's supposed to do.

Step 3: Implement the Strategy

I'll follow my strategy until the behavior becomes automatic. *If your motivation and willpower are weak, make strengthening those your goals and implement a strategy. (See Chapters 9 and 10.)*

Note: For all habits, first establish the habit in a nondistracting environment. For example, start out on quiet streets and then, over time, work up to busier streets with more distractions such as other animals, more traffic, etc.

Step 4: Maintain the New Habit

Once the new habit is established, it's important to maintain it by doing it consistently over a period of time. Repetition and time are both needed to solidify the behavior. Because you developed the habit to step on the leash *each time* you stop walking, he has had to stop too. Therefore, the "sit when you stop walking" behavior is maintained and reinforced.

Dogs are very economical. They only do what works and they stop doing anything that doesn't work. Once the behavior becomes reliable in that particular situation, it's simply a matter of teaching her to sit in other environments (with distractions like other dogs) and after that, you will only occasionally have to ask for a sit or stand on the leash again.

Once a behavior is installed as a habit, it becomes automatic.

Don't keep opening the oven to see if the meal is cooked. Believe in your strategy and the habits you're using. You'll get there.

Part 2

The 7-Day Vacation for Canine Education

Chapter 6

Taking a Vacation for Canine Education

Over a period of thirty-five years, I used every motivational method I could come up with to help people integrate and practice what they learned in my group classes, which usually run for six weeks. I wanted people to WANT to train their dogs because it was fun and rewarding. I didn't want people to feel that training was a chore and something they HAD to do.

So, along with the dog games, I used people games and people rewards and all kinds of stuff to motivate everybody to return to class each week. Over time I steadied out with a really good attendance record. But, invariably, I'd lose two or three people before the six-week session ended and I always took that as a challenge. I wanted to have as many people finish the session as started, factoring in attrition due to health issues and emergencies, of course.

It all turned around and my attendance record jumped and remained high, start-to-finish, when I changed my approach.

Here is what I now tell people the first week in class: DO NOT ASK YOUR DOG TO SIT, LIE DOWN, GET HIS TOY, GO TO HIS SPOT, COME, OR STAY FOR THE NEXT SEVEN DAYS.

Yup. I suggest taking a vacation from *asking* your dog to do any of these things. Don't *ask* for a sit, down, stay, or come and don't use any vocal or hand signals of any kind, except those needed to play some games, which are described in Chapter 7. The best way to learn a totally new way to communicate is to stand back, take a breather, and look at things from a new perspective. So even if your dog knows these behaviors very well, don't ask for them during the seven days. This 7-day program will revolutionize how you talk to your dog and firmly establish the foundation for the habit training that you'll institute beginning on day eight, which is found in Chapter 8.

A 7-Day Crash Course in Dogspeak

Why take this 7-day vacation? One of the biggest problems people have with training their puppies and dogs is the underlying sense that the puppy or dog speaks English—or whatever human language they speak. The reality is that people don't speak dog; they've never acquired the skills needed to really communicate with their dog. The Vacation for Canine Education program is a weeklong crash course in dogspeak. There is no quicker way to begin to learn what your dog is saying and why your dog does what she does than by being forced to observe her rather than nag her.

It's not that dogs just have to learn our language, we have to learn *their* way of communicating. And miscommunications abound. For example, what exactly does the dog mean when he wags his tail? Every trainer I know has heard the same refrain from clients who were bitten by their own dogs: "I thought he was friendly because his tail was wagging." That's sometimes true but a wagging tail can mean something else entirely. Maybe he's distressed or maybe he's displaying submissive behavior. Then again, maybe he's aggressive. It depends on the position, speed, and tension of the wagging tail. What if a dog is showing teeth? Is that always a sign of aggression? Heck, no. Maybe he's happy and smiling.

I visit many homes each week for private dog training sessions. Most of these visits deal with problem behaviors, which range from extremely fearful dogs to extremely aggressive dogs and everything in between. Ninety percent of these clients have "had dogs all their life." And yet, when they attend classes and learn the basics in dog communication, even the most savvy dog lover is often amazed to learn what their dogs were actually doing and saying to them all those years.

Stop Ineffective Communication and Learn Effective Communication

How can a typical human possibly understand their dog when they are constantly "barking" at him? ("Sit." "Sit." "Sit." "Down." "Down. "Down." "No." "No." "No.") The key is to observe the dog and become aware of what he is communicating. Certainly books, DVDs, and seminars can be a huge help in learning dogspeak, but a more sure-fire way to learn is by silent observation and experimentation. Taking a vacation for canine education gives you just that opportunity. Specifically, for seven days, you are going to remain silent every time your dog offers a behavior that you're NOT looking for and reward only those behaviors you ARE looking for.

When this program is implemented, the first thing that will happen is a dramatic reduction in the level of stress—both for you and your puppy or dog. As soon as you "go on vacation" and stop *trying* to train your dog, you will relax and so will your dog. You will be able to predict with increasing skill what your dog will do, when she will do it, and how she will do it. With that knowledge, you can quickly learn to anticipate problems before they happen and proactively redirect her behavior rather than reactively using punishment to try to stop her from repeating the behavior you don't want. A dog's stress level dramatically decreases when she can predict the likely consequences of her behavior. In other words, the only time a dog "gets into trouble" is when the dog was given too much freedom too soon and was never taught and told what TO DO instead.

The 7-Day Program

On the 7-Day Vacation for Canine Education program, you will do basically the same things you do on a leisurely tropical vacation:

1. Practice safety and be polite.
2. Play and have fun.
3. Take photos (well, in this case, it's a different type of photo, as you'll see below).

Here are the details of the 7-day vacation for canine education:

Practice Safety and Be Polite

Although you won't be asking your puppy or dog to do anything during this 7-day vacation other than play games (which I'll get to in a moment), safety is paramount. Stealing, destructive chewing, bolting out the door, jumping on people, and so on are not only obnoxious behaviors, there's also a potential for injury to your dog or a person. So some rules to prevent problems and properly manage your dog are imperative. In reality, these are safety rules that should be followed with any training method:

- The house must be dog-proof. Prevent stealing and chewing problems by making sure all illegal objects such as shoes, children's toys, the TV remote, plants, and anything else of value are out of reach.
- If your dog pulls or lunges on walks, use an anti-pulling collar or harness. (See page 37.)
- Tether your dog using a leash, baby gate, or kennel so your dog is not able to jump on people when they come in the house, dig in the garden, or be destructive. *For safety, never tether a dog unless he is supervised.* When you are watching TV, spending time on the computer, eating or relaxing, tether your dog nearby and give her something great to chew on and to keep busy. For those dogs who are more trouble free, more free time is offered. (See how to tether on page 41.)

Tethering Your Puppy or Dog to You

If your puppy or dog is completely out of control, chewing, jumping, and eliminating, tether her to you by attaching her leash to your belt or around your waist while you're in the house. This method can be very helpful in resolving these problems. It's as if you had an umbilical cord connecting the two of you so that she must go where you go. And it's not possible for her to get into trouble because she's always with you.

Play and Have Fun

I cannot emphasize enough the importance of playing with your puppy or dog and this is especially true on the 7-day vacation. The neat thing is that play fulfills a dog's requirements for exercise and play at the same time. Playing exercises your dog's mind and emotions, as well as her body. Games relieve stress and help create a trusting bond between you and your dog. During the 7-day vacation, you'll also focus on playing Find It, Tug, and Fetch, which are taught in the next chapter. In fact, the Find It game is one of the most powerful ways for you to learn "dogspeak." Simply by playing Find It, your dog's confidence will increase dramatically and she will increasingly focus her attention on you. During the 7-day vacation, Find It, Tug, and Fetch are the only "behaviors" for which you will give your dog vocal cues by *asking* for the behavior.

Take Photos by Playing the Magnet Game

Just as a picture is "captured" by a camera, a puppy or dog's appropriate behavior is metaphorically "captured" by giving praise and a treat the instant that behavior happens. Dogs quickly get the idea and begin repeating whatever behavior they get the most rewards for. Behaviors you *want* get rewarded and behaviors you *don't want* are ignored.

Another name I use for this concept is the "Magnet Game." Just as a magnet attracts metal, the desired behavior attracts praise and food treats. The faster you respond to her appropriate behaviors with praise and treats, the clearer it will be to her that you are praising and rewarding her for the behavior she just did.

Figure 6-1

The magnet game consists of waiting for your dog to figure out what you want without you having to ask for it. In this photo, Orbit, a Chinese crested, is being ignored because she is standing up on her bed.

Figure 6-2

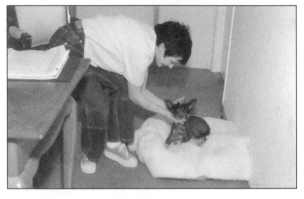

As soon as Orbit lies down without being told, she is immediately rewarded with praise, treats, and affection.

At the same time that you are "capturing" and rewarding behaviors you want to reinforce, you are ignoring all inappropriate behaviors, unless those behaviors are unsafe, self-reinforcing, or destructive. By capturing and rewarding behaviors you are teaching your dog what you want her to do in the way your dog understands. You will be amazed how quickly your dog picks up on this.

Why is this method so effective? Dogs are very economical and precise. This is the number one reason that the canine vacation is so powerful. If something they are doing doesn't get them what they want, they will stop doing it. It's just that simple. If jumping, barking, nose-nuzzling, and pawing doesn't work but sitting or lying down does, they will stop doing what doesn't work and start offering behaviors that do. Dogs often continue to offer inappropriate behaviors because they are often unintentionally rewarded by the human. For example, if a dog jumps on someone and the person pushes him off and yells "No," the jumping may have actually been reinforced because of all the attention the dog got. Unless the push was really intense and the "NO" really loud, those two things actually reinforced the jumping. Or if a person is yelling at the dog to stop barking, the yelling may be reinforcing the barking. Why? Because, to a dog, the person is joining in on the barking.

> Do not ignore unsafe, self-reinforcing, or destructive behaviors. Follow the suggestions in the section, "Practice Safety and Be Polite" on page 73.

There are five behaviors you will be concentrating on during your vacation. Remember, you are not *asking* for these behaviors; you are rewarding your dog when she does the behavior without being asked. Each of these behaviors will be "captured" by instantly rewarding your dog when it occurs with praise, petting, affection, life rewards (see page 155), and treats.

The Five Behaviors to "Capture" Using the Magnet Game

🦴 **Sit:** Whenever you see your dog sit, instantly reward with praise (say "good" or "yay" or "yes"), and give a treat. This is especially effective when your dog is tethered.

🦴 **Down:** Whenever you see your dog lie down, instantly reward with praise (say "good" or "yay" or "yes"), petting, and give several treats. This is especially effective when your dog is tethered.

- **Goes to her bed:** Whenever you see your dog go to her bed, instantly reward with praise (say "good" or "yay" or "yes"), and give *many* treats.

- **Looks to you for direction:** Whenever your dog looks to you for direction, especially when she looks away from an "illegal" object like food on the table or slippers, instantly reward with praise (say "good" or "yay" or "yes"), petting, and give treats.

- **Brings a dog toy to you:** Whenever your dog brings a toy to you, instantly reward with praise (say "good" or "yay" or "yes"), and throw the toy or initiate a game of Tug.

When you are watching TV, spending time on the computer, eating or relaxing, tether your dog nearby and give her something great to chew on and keep busy. During these times, you will be "taking a photo" and capturing the desired behaviors of sit, down, or looking to you for direction or comfort. Capturing a behavior is done by instantly acknowledging the sit or the down with praise, petting, and giving the highest quality food treats the instant it happens.

Figure 6-3

The Five Behaviors to "Capture" Using the Magnet Game

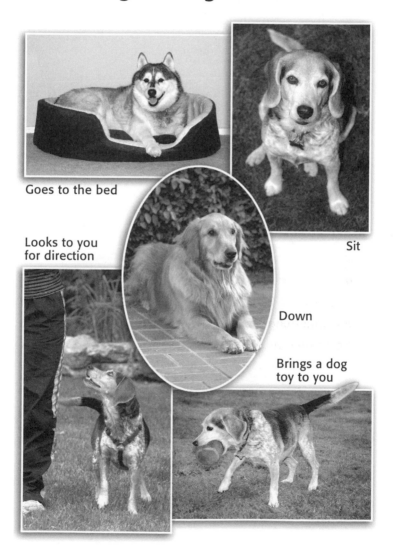

Goes to the bed

Sit

Looks to you
for direction

Down

Brings a dog
toy to you

Vacation Timeline

As I explained before, it generally takes twenty-eight days to form a new habit; however, by jump-starting your habit training with the 7-Day Vacation for Canine Education, you will see even more dramatic results when you actually start asking your dog to do something.

Rewarding Continuous Behavior

If you only give your dog one food treat when capturing any behavior, such as when he lies down, he might quickly pop up again. Every once in a while, quickly throw a second treat or even a third while he is still lying down, as if to say, "Oh, you're still down? Well, I like that, so here's another treat! And here's another treat!" Your dog will quickly learn to stay in the sit or down position longer and longer, anticipating more treats. Gradually you can progress to weaning your dog off treats and all that will be necessary is an occasional pat on the head and a big "That'll do, Pal."

The purpose of the 7-Day Vacation for Canine Education is to have fun with your dog, improve your communication, and strengthen the bond between you and her.

You will find that *your* actions become more and more automatic and precise. Each time you catch your puppy or dog in the act of looking to you, going to her bed, sitting or lying down, you'll find yourself automatically rewarding her without even thinking about it. As your actions become more and more automatic, so will your dog's.

To summarize, you are not *asking* your dog to sit, lie down, stay, look at you, go to her bed, or come while on your Canine Vacation. Find It, Tug, and Fetch are the only "behaviors" you are allowed to use a word for during the 7-day vacation. Every other behavior your dog offers (sit, down, look, go to bed, or bringing you a toy) is acknowledged and rewarded but is never requested. That being the case, how and when do you start using the words "sit," "down," etc. to get your dog to do what you ask him to do? The answer to that is found in Chapter 8.

Have fun!

Chapter 7

Games to Play on Vacation—
Find It, Tug, and Fetch

Telling a child to "stop crying" doesn't work because crying is a symptom. Deal with the cause as to why the child is crying (fear, frustration, etc.) and the symptom disappears. The same holds true with having fun. Telling someone to "have fun" when they're not especially motivated is worthless. We all need to feel like something's fun, not be told that it is. So the trick to motivate yourself is by experimenting and see what happens. The proof is in the pudding. If the following suggestions work, you won't need to be told to "have fun." Sometimes the simplest games can be the most powerful in developing great temperament and reliable behavior. Find It, Tug, and Fetch are the perfect examples. They're easy, they're fun, they're practical and they can be used to resolve a host of problems including chewing, jumping, running away, barking, not coming when called, and more. (See Chapter 8.) Most importantly, they help form a terrific bond of trust between you and your dog so he ends up wanting to do things with you rather than feeling the stress of being forced.

Find It, Tug, and Fetch are the only behaviors you'll be teaching your puppy or dog to do by actually using vocal or hand signals (commands) during the 7-day vacation. All other behaviors like sit, down, stay, come, go-to-bed and so on during this 7-day period are taught without signals.

Here's a final note: Attitude helps. If you're relaxed, smiling, singing, and dancing, your dog relaxes and happily remains open to whatever you have to teach him. If you're having fun, your dog's having fun.

The "Find It" Trilogy

Find It is actually a series of three separate games. The Find It games are simple, easy to habituate, and incredibly powerful. Let me emphasize again that these are games.

The purpose of the Find It games is to:

- Redirect your puppy or dog's attention away from Mother Nature's treasure chest of distractions and increase his focus and attention on you;
- Build a stronger bond and trust with you;
- Increase his confidence;
- Teach him to relax no matter what life throws at him;
- Teach him a substitute (replacement) behavior for any inappropriate or unwanted behavior.

Needed for all Find It games:

- Highly valued and varied treats, preferably in a fanny pack around your waist for easy and quick access
- A happy, fun disposition

Find It #1: Throwing the Treat

1. Get your dog's attention by saying his name or making a "kissy" sound, whistling, or making some other sound with your mouth. If he's distracted by something else, move yourself to a less distracting environment. You can also get his attention by moving your hand with a highly valued treat in front of his nose.
2. The instant your dog looks at you, say "Find it" and throw the treat three or four feet to the side. Repeat this ten times.

Do ten or so repetitions in each session and practice several times throughout the day.

The object is to get an automatic response from your dog so whenever you say "Find it" he will immediately turn away from whatever he's looking at and start looking for the treat. In most cases, he should start doing this within a week in non-distracting environments. However, your dog's reliability with Find It, that is the point the behavior becomes automatic, will depend on his history, how many times you practice it, his connection with you, and many other factors. That being said, the habit of him automatically looking for the treat whenever he hears "Find it" should form in twenty-eight days.

Figure 7-1

In step 2 of Find It #1, the instant your dog looks at you, say "Find it" and throw the treat three or four feet to the side.

Do not ignore unsafe, self-reinforcing, or destructive behaviors. Follow the suggestions in the section, "Practice Safety and Be Polite" on page 73.

Practice this game indoors and outdoors. Unless you're in a fenced yard, your puppy or dog will, of course, be on a leash. Experiment with different treats and times of day. He'll have more motivation if he's a bit hungry, so it's better to practice before rather than after his meals.

Once your dog knows the game and eagerly awaits your next throw, you can begin to associate it with more and more distractions. For example, if your puppy or dog is nervous about people or other dogs when you go for a walk, play the Find It game by saying the phrase and immediately throwing the treat as the distraction comes into view. Over time your dog will start turning to you and away from the distraction. When that happens, two things are taking place:

1. The treat is being associated with the distraction and you are changing the way he feels about it. In other words, the stimulus (other dog or human) is now being associated not only with a treat but also with a game. With enough repetitions over a period of time, your dog will come to love the distraction!

2. The second thing that's happening is that you are teaching your dog to turn away from the distraction and pay attention to you. This will then become a habit; whenever another dog or person appears, your dog will automatically look to you or turn his head to the ground looking for treats. You have thus successfully substituted a desired behavior (paying attention to you and hunting for treats) for an undesired behavior (chasing dogs or people).

The instructions for Find It sound simple, don't they? Yet sometimes a dog won't chase the treat. Why? The number one reason is that he's distracted and the solution is usually to move to a less distracting environment. But your goal is to learn to redirect your dog's attention away from the distraction.

Let's look at the process your dog goes through when a distraction appears. Most dogs will take the time to ascertain whether they should fight, freeze, or run away. Your job is to immediately interrupt that process and have him focus on you instead. To do that, it's helpful to be aware of the four progressive stages a dog goes through. By becoming aware of these stages, you can learn to redirect your dog's attention right away, while he's still at the first stage, which is "alert" and thereby avoid potential problems.

1. **Alert:** The alert stage is when your dog sees the approaching stimulus and starts garnering all information he can about whether the thing is safe or a threat. You'll see his ears perk up and turn forward, his body will lean forward and he'll be sniffing the air like mad.
2. **Stillness:** In the stillness stage, his focus will really hone in as his decision to move toward or away from the stimulus becomes more acute. His tail will be perfectly still or, if it is moving, it will be slow.
3. **Stiffness:** The third stage is stiffness. You can actually feel this stage as the dog almost becomes a statue.
4. **Trigger:** In the next instant, he'll either bolt toward or away from the stimulus.

Whenever you play the Find It game, your intention is to be far enough away from the distraction so your dog can be redirected in the alert stage. Once he goes to stage two or three, you won't be able to get him to pay attention to you. It means you're too close or simply not ready to take the show on the road. In situations like these, it's okay to pull him away to increase your distance, but be sure that you don't jerk him. And keep your affect upbeat, perhaps with words like, "C'mon, Pal, let's go this way," or words to that effect.

Other Reasons Your Puppy or Dog Won't Play the Find It Game	
Maybe you threw the treat too fast or too far. This is especially true for young puppies.	Solution: Make your throws more deliberate. Throw the treat to the side and not behind your dog. Keep the treat within your dog's peripheral vision.
Maybe he's motion sensitive and is nervous about your hand motion.	Solution: Make your throws slower, more deliberate, and less intense.
Maybe he's just confused.	Solution: Make sure he sees you throw the treat and throw it no more than six inches away.
Maybe the treat isn't valuable enough.	Solution: Upgrade to a food treat that is more "valuable" to your dog, such as chicken, cheese, etc.

If your puppy or dog is sensitive or fearful:

When walking a sensitive or fearful puppy or dog, use an anti-pulling collar or harness rather than attaching the leash to the collar. I recommend Easy Walk, Sensation, Halti Headcollar, Halti Harness, Gentle Leader, and K9 Bridle, which is made in England.

Find It as a Problem Solver

As simple as the game of Find It is, it is a powerful remedy for three of the most common problems: pulling on a leash, not coming when called, and jumping.

Using Find It #1 for Dogs Who Pull on Walks

While on a walk with your dog, say "Find it" and throw the treat behind you. Repeat this several dozen times on each walk and, within a month's time, where do you think your dog will start hanging out? Exactly, behind you. This then becomes the substitute behavior for dogs who pull. If you want, you can rename this behavior "Get in back" or "Get behind me" instead of "Find It."

Figure 7-2

To teach your dog to walk without pulling, practice Find It by throwing a treat behind you while on a walk.

Using Find It #1 to Get Your Dog to Come

Another use for Find It #1 is getting your dog to come in from the yard. Let's say you're ready to go to work but your dog is in the backyard having a good old time with a ball. In the past, you would say, "Come" and he ignored you. Now, you say "Find it" and drop the treat at your feet. If you've been practicing the Find It game, he'll come to get the treat. So "Find it" means "come."

Figure 7-3

Use Find It to get your dog to come when called by saying "Find it" and throwing a treat at your feet.

91

Using Find It #1 as a Substitute for Jumping

Another use for Find It is as a substitute for jumping. Let's say you have a dog that jumps on you whenever you come in the house. Anticipating this behavior, you now arm yourself with treats in your pocket or fanny pack and get some treats out as you approach the door. As you open the door, say "Find it" before he has a chance to jump on you. As he runs to get the treat, you start walking across the room. Then, before he has a chance to jump, once again you say "Find it" and throw another treat. Continue walking and throwing more treats as you cross the room. Within a week your dog will automatically back up in anticipation of you throwing the treat instead of jumping on you. Now how easy is that!

Figure 7-4

Use Find It to solve a jumping problem by throwing a treat off to the side before your dog jumps.

Note: For more information about other substitute behaviors for jumping, read *The Dog Whisperer* and *The Puppy Whisperer* or get my DVD, *The Dog Whisperer—Vol. 2: Solving Common Behavior Problems for Puppies and Dogs.*

Find It #2: Hiding the Treat

This is one of the easiest games to play with your puppy or dog and yet one of the most powerful and quickest ways to make the transition into a new home as stress-free as possible, desensitize a dog to motion, and get a dog to really keep his attention on you.

1. With your dog no more than three feet from you and a highly valued treat in your hand, get your dog's attention.
2. As soon as he looks at you, say "Find it" and let him see you place the treat behind something. This can be a wall, a shoe, a chair leg, a flower pot, anything.
3. Now wait. Give him a chance to consider this new opportunity. If he starts sniffing the ground, he should find the treat within forty-five seconds.
4. Praise him heartily and show him another hiding spot. Once again say "Find it" and let him see you place the treat behind something else. When he finds that treat, praise him again and one more time, follow the same routine with yet another hiding spot. It's like a treasure hunt and you're showing him where you're hiding the treasure.

5. Once your dog is reliable up to step 4, you're going to up the ante. Follow the same routine but this time, when he finds the hidden treat, run with goofy, exaggerated sounds and motion to the next location. When you stop at the new location and he looks at you, once again say "Find it," and place a treat there. Then goofily run to another location. This second goofy run should be different than the previous one and might include arm waving, foot stomping, and yelling "woo woo."

Figure 7-5

In Find It #2, teach your dog to find a treat with his nose by first getting his attention, then say "Find it" and let him see you place a treat behind something.

To redirect your dog's attention away from joggers and kids on bikes and skateboards, use Find It #2 to teach him to hunt with his nose while adding distractions, like goofy sounds and motions.

So what's going on here? In Find It #2, you are teaching your dog to pay attention to you. Second, you are desensitizing him to strange movements and sounds. If your dog is frightened when you, someone he is familiar with and trusts, moves around, you can't expect him to relax on the street when kids whiz by on skateboards or a funny-looking bald guy (see any photo of me) jogs by. Once you've taught your dog to associate goofy movements with the Find It game, ask other members of your family to do the same thing. When your dog associates the strange movements and sounds of your family with treats, he will then begin to generalize. He will no longer be frightened when other people move in similar fashions. Instead of chasing them or running away from them, he'll think that they must be playing the Find It game too. And true to form, whenever an unexpected event occurs, such as a jogger or skateboarder going by, you will be the one throwing the treats and saying, "Find it."

This simple game increases your dog's confidence, counter-conditions him to frightening movements, and redirects his attention to you. But that's not all. Let's say you've been practicing Find It #2 for twenty-eight days and by now your dog knows fifty different hiding spots. You've shown him treats being hidden behind chairs, the ottoman, the desk, the couch, the door—and even in other rooms.

Note: To add more time to the game, instead of just putting one treat in each hiding spot, hide a Bully stick, treat-filled Kong, and /or a chicken breast strip in one or more of the spots. That'll keep him busy so he has something else to do for even longer periods of time instead of chewing furniture or digging in the garden.

If Your Puppy or Dog Is Confused

If your puppy or dog is confused and simply cannot figure out what you are trying to teach him, always back up to a step that he can understand. For example, place the treat right in front of him several times, so he can associate the phrase "Find it" with the treats. Then let him see you place the treats behind something that's closer to his nose—no more than six inches away. This is why dogs respond more quickly to real food like chicken than dry treats—the smell is stronger.

For Motion-Sensitive Puppies or Dogs

If your puppy or dog is motion sensitive, relax the intensity of the goofy movements. Walk to and from each hiding-place location at a pace your dog can handle and gradually increase the intensity of your movements as the days and weeks go by.

Using Find It #2 as a Substitute for Inappropriate Behaviors

Find It #2 can be a good way to get your dog to stop barking, begging, chewing, and other unwanted behaviors. Now try this. Ask your dog to lie down and stay. Leave the room and put treats in ten to twenty familiar locations in another room. Return to your dog and say, "Find it." There will initially be some confusion, but wait. Your dog will soon run into the other room and start hunting. He'll be busy for fifteen minutes with his new job. In the meantime, you can go take a shower, read the newspaper, or have breakfast while he does his thing. You are now on your way to substituting this hunting behavior for barking at people on the street, begging at the table, chewing bunny slippers, and a host of other inappropriate behaviors.

Find It #3: Peek-a-Boo

There is no easier way to form a strong bond of trust with your dog, have fun, and redirect your dog's attention to you—all at the same time—than playing Peek-a-boo. Peek-a-boo, sometimes called Hide-and-seek, is the greatest fun your dog can have with you as it combines physical, mental, and emotional stimulation. In addition, as you'll read at the end of the instructions, it has a practical application because it can literally save your dog's life.

The key to a successful game of Peek-a-boo is to make it all-but-impossible for your dog not to succeed. This means take baby steps.

1. Get your dog's attention as with Find It #1 and #2.
2. As soon as your dog glances at you, say "Find it" and throw the treat as you learned in Find It #1.
3. As your dog runs to the treat, scoot behind the nearest chair, couch or wall.
4. Then stick your head out and let your dog see you. When he does, happily exclaim "Peek-a-boo" and quickly tuck your head out of sight. When your dog shows up to find you, happily and excitedly exclaim, "Oh you found me! How awesome a hunter you are!" and lavish treats, praise, and petting on him.
5. Now repeat the routine but hide somewhere else. Make sure your dog sees you before tucking your head out of sight. If your dog doesn't see you, make a "kissy" sound or other distracting noise to help orient him to your location.

6. Then repeat this same sequence again in another location.

Figure 7-7

In Peek-a-boo, hide from your dog. Then stick your head out and let her see you. Enthusiastically say, "Peek-a-boo" and tuck your head out of sight.

Figure 7-8

Once you are hidden, your dog will start looking for you.

Figure 7-9

When your puppy finds you, praise and treat her.

As time goes by, you can play this game for up to five minutes but I recommend a shorter duration when you first start teaching him. Three or four shorter sequences will do.

If Your Puppy or Dog Is Skittish

If you have a skittish puppy or dog who refuses to even come close to where you're hiding, stay hidden but throw a highly valued treat half way to the dog. Repeat this but next time throw the treat a little closer to your location. Soon your dog will see you hiding and you can show your pleasure and appreciation but keep the celebration to a level of intensity he can handle.

After a day or two, when your dog realizes what the Peek-a-boo game is all about, sneak away while he is preoccupied with something else like looking out the window and hide in one of the previously designated locations. Then yell "Peek-a-boo" loud enough for him to hear, but don't let him see where you're hiding. He will excitedly run around the house or yard until he finds you. When he does, once again make a huge deal out of the fact he was so smart and "jackpot" him with lots of praise, petting, and treats. Keep the game easy in the beginning by hiding in known places. Don't hide in a closet with the door closed until he has figured out how to use his nose to find you. The first few weeks he'll use his eyes but eventually he'll automatically switch to using his nose to track you down. Then you can close the closet door and open it when you hear him outside it, again rewarding him with praise, petting, and treats.

As I mentioned, Peek-a-boo is the ultimate dog-human bonding game. But it can actually be used to save your puppy or dog's life. Let's say you've been playing "Peek-a-boo" for six months or so and have gotten a thousand or so Peek-a-boo games under your belt. Now your dog has formed a powerful habit. Whenever he hears the sound of you saying "Peek-a-boo," he immediately begins to orient and starts trying to find you.

Now imagine, God forbid, that someone forgot to close the front door and he bolts out the door after a cat, squirrel, or other dog and he's headed for the street. You scream "Come" but he ignores you and keeps running. Now yell "Peek-a-boo!" The chances of him turning toward you when he hears that sound are greatly increased. The reason for this is because people are not as consistent in teaching "come" nor do they play "come" with the same joy and enthusiasm as Peek-a-boo. In this scenario, when your dog glances back at you, start running crazily down the street with the same goofy running that you used in Find It #2. While doing this, yell "Peek-a-boo, Peek-a-boo." Your dog, with just a little luck, will come running after you as fast as he can. Peek-a-boo becomes an emergency recall.

Note: You can use any word or phrase you want instead of "Peek-a-boo," such as "Bingo," "Cookie," or whatever you like. I use "Peek-a-boo" because I work with a lot of children.

Playing Tug

Tug is another game that is played whenever you want on the 7-Day Canine Vacation. It will teach your dog the vitally important concept of "give and take." Here are some guidelines that will make it easy and fun. In Level Two, Advanced Tug, you'll also include "drop it," which is also known as "let go."

Note: Some puppies and dogs pick up on this game immediately and are happy to put the toy in their mouth and play Tug with you. If that's the case, you can proceed to level two immediately. The whole idea of the game is to get your dog to put her mouth on the toy and hold it until asked to release it.

Level One: Beginning Tug

1. Rub a piece of chicken or turkey on a ball or other toy that you want your dog to take. Hold the ball one inch

from your dog's nose and give the verbal signal "Take it."

2. When your dog touches the ball with his nose, praise, and feed a $10,000 treat. Repeat five to ten times.

3. When your dog figures out that he'll get a treat whenever he touches the ball with his nose, lower it an inch closer to the floor when you present it and repeat the process. How do you know your dog has figured it out? If he touches the ball within three seconds after you said "take it." Your goal is to progress by lowering the ball inch-by-inch to a point that he will touch the object when you place it the floor. Depending on the breed of dog and his age and experience, this may take several sessions. Don't rush it.

Note: At this point, your dog is not actually "taking" the ball, he's just touching it with his nose. However, some dogs may immediately put the object in their mouth, which is your ultimate goal. If that happens, you can start playing Tug immediately. When she grasps the toy, verbally encourage her to play. While you and your dog are hanging on to the toy, move it back and forth, and up and down. Allow the Tug session to continue for ten to twenty seconds. Then you can skip the steps 4, 5, and 6 below because you're ready to go to Level Two: Advanced Tug, with "Drop It" or "Let Go," where you'll be asking her to drop it.

Figure 7-10

In step 6 of Beginning Tug, increase the amount of time your dog holds on to the object before you praise and treat.

4. If your dog is consistently touching the ball whenever you point to it on the floor, it's time to up the ante. Place the ball on the floor and say "Take it." When he touches it, praise him but don't give him a treat. Wait for him to escalate the behavior by nudging, licking or even taking the object in his mouth. If he does any of these things, quickly praise and treat. Here's what's happening. When your dog touches the object and is rewarded with praise but not rewarded with a treat, he will try to figure out why the food reward does not follow. In essence, he's thinking, "Wait a minute, we had a deal! You're supposed to give me a treat every time

I touch the object. Well, I'll show you!" He will then naturally escalate his intensity by licking, nudging, or mouthing the object. It is that escalation that you are now rewarding. So wait until your dog licks or nudges the object. When he does, praise and treat. Repeat five to ten times.

5. After a few sessions, you'll up the ante again by once again praising him for his current behavior (licking or nudging) but withholding the food reward. And once again he will escalate his behavior by actually picking the ball up. When he does, enthusiastically praise and repeat until he actually holds onto the ball. When that happens, start playing Tug.

HINT: You can speed this process by asking your dog to "Take it" when you throw a $10,000 treat or a favorite toy toward him. Many dogs will automatically "catch" something that's thrown to them.

6. Gradually progress to a point where your dog will hold the ball for longer periods of time. This is done by simply increasing the amount of time your dog holds the object before you praise and treat. Hold on to the toy and move it back and forth (do not jerk) and continue playing Tug for ten to twenty seconds. Now ask for your dog to let it go or say "Drop it." Here's how that's done.

Level Two: Advanced Tug, with "Drop It" or "Let Go"

Up until now, you've allowed him to hold on to it for as long as he likes. Now you are going to teach him to "drop it" ("let go") and willingly give the toy back to you when you ask for it.

1. Have some tasty treats tucked in your pocket or in a container on a nearby shelf. Start playing Tug with your dog,

2. Hold a treat in the hand that is not holding the toy. After ten to twenty seconds of gently playing Tug, say "Drop it" and show your dog the treat. He probably will let go of the toy. When he does, immediately give him the treat. Continue to hold the toy with the hand that was not holding the treat. (See Figure 7-11.)

3. Repeat the whole sequence, beginning with "Okay" and following with "Drop it" and showing a treat after ten to twenty seconds of play. You can repeat this many times in a single play session.

Figure 7-11

When playing Tug, to get your dog to release the toy, say "Drop it" or "Let go" and present a treat. When he drops the toy, give him the treat.

If Your Dog Doesn't Let Go of the Toy for a Treat

Some dogs prefer holding on to a toy, even if you present a treat. Sometimes you can solve this problem by increasing the value of the treat, using chicken, turkey, or cheese. Other dogs are generally more interested in toys than food and will let go of one toy in exchange for another. Try pulling another toy out of your pocket instead of a treat to see if that's the case with your dog. If all else fails, you can hold completely still until your dog gives up and lets go. When you do this, be as quiet as possible—don't talk to your dog, look at your dog, or move too much.

If Your Dog Loses Interest in Playing

Some dogs will catch on right away that they are getting a treat in exchange for a toy. They might decide that the treats are much more interesting than the toy, and they might stop playing altogether and just stare at you, waiting for more treats. If that happens, put the toy away for at least a few minutes and start playing again later. If your dog is still more interested in the treats than in the toys, it's time to graduate to a "drop it" or "let go" without treats (see below).

"Drop It" ("Let Go") Without Treats

In the beginning, you will have to teach your dog "Drop It" using food treats. But it shouldn't take too long before your dog lets go of the toy as soon as he hears "drop it" or "let go," without seeing a treat. In fact, you may notice that your dog starts automatically letting go of the toy, without waiting to be asked. Now is the time to change the nature of your cooperation. If your dog gives up the toy, the reward is that you keep playing! The prize for letting go of the toy is to let him grab it in his mouth again. Sparky is learning to let go, because he trusts that you will give it back again. He is learning that he can give up in order to get. What a great lesson.

Ask for the toy back many times during a play session, as "payment" for the continuation of play, like putting another quarter in a parking meter. If at any point he refuses to let go when asked, hold still and try to be as boring and lifeless as possible. Do this until he lets go, at which point you become animated and playful again. He will learn quickly that if he wants you to play with him, you will only do so if he cooperates. If he is cooperating well and you would like to end the play session, you can reward his final return of the toy with a treat. This way the end of the play session is not a punishment.

Once your dog knows how to drop the the toy, you can use Tug as a "life reward" instead of using treats. Let's say you're playing a session of Tug and say "Drop it." Immediately ask your dog to sit or lie down. As soon as she does, start playing Tug again. The reward for sitting or lying down is the continuation of the game. But what happens if your dog doesn't sit and jumps on you or tries to grab the toy?

Problem Solving

If your dog jumps up, tries to grab the toy out of your hand, barks, pulls on your sleeve, or does any other obnoxious behavior, calmly put the toy behind your back. If your dog sits or lies down, present it to her again, in the same way you did before. If she waits patiently for two seconds, say "Okay," give her the toy, and start gently tugging. If she grabs for it, put the toy calmly behind your back. Repeat this sequence until your dog waits for the toy without grabbing until you give her permission.

After several repetitions of this you will probably notice that your dog starts waiting patiently. She is learning that jumping, grabbing, barking, and so on make the toy disappear. Gradually, you can start increasing the amount of time that you would like your dog to wait patiently, from two seconds to three, then five, etc. and start playing. If she jumps or mouths you at any point when you are playing Tug, institute "Time Out," which is described later in this chapter. (See "Time Out" on page 112.)

If Your Dog Isn't Interested in the Toy

🦴 Some dogs seem to need to "learn" how to play. Attitude is everything here. If you are excited, upbeat, and playful, it is more likely your dog will start feeling that way too. Try playing this variation of Peek-a-boo: Hold a toy and hide from your dog. Let the toy stick out from your hiding place so your dog can see it. When your dog finds you, move the toy around excitedly on the ground, as if it was a small animal.

🦴 Some dogs prefer playing with toys that squeak or make sounds. Find what your dog likes best and use that for your Tug games. If your dog is timid and/or sensitive to motion and sound, be calmer when you move the toy. Anytime your dog makes any movement toward the toy or touches it with her nose, encourage her with praise and treats. As she starts to show more interest, she may put her mouth on the toy for a moment, then a little bit longer, etc. Reward each of these baby steps with praise and treats.

Fetch

Now it's your turn to apply the lessons of Tug to games that include throwing a ball, Frisbee, or other toy. You are going to teach yourself to let go of the toy and trust that your dog will give it back. In Tug games, the toy is always in your hand, which is a good way to begin establishing the habit of cooperation.

If Your Dog Isn't Interested in Fetch

Some dogs love to play Tug, but don't seem to enjoy going after a toy and picking it up. Try holding on to the toy on the floor, a couple of feet away from your body, and moving it around with an excited and upbeat attitude. If your dog takes the toy in her mouth, let go of the toy and clap your hands to get her to bring it the one or two feet back to you. You can also place the toy on the floor, right in front of your dog, and reward her with praise and treats if she looks at it. Continue this routine until she touches the toy with her nose, then takes it in her mouth, etc. Reward each of these baby steps along the way. Be patient—it can take many sessions—and keep a fun attitude.

1. Holding a ball in front of you at chest level, repeat the same waiting patiently routine that you practiced with Tug. Only now, instead of letting your dog take it in his mouth, say "Fetch" or "Take it" and toss the ball a foot or two in front of you. Keep it a very short distance for the moment.

2. Wait for your dog to pick up the ball and bring it back to you. She will probably do this right away, since she has developed cooperative play habits with Tug games. But if she doesn't bring it back, don't move toward her to get it. You risk making it into a chase game if you move toward your dog at this point. Trust that she will bring it back. If she doesn't come back after forty-five seconds, run away from her. You can say "Peek-a-boo," call her name, or make excited sounds. This will definitely bring her to you, further developing his habit of coming back to you with the toy.

3. Each time your dog comes back to you, she will probably automatically drop the ball. If she doesn't, simply go through the same steps for "Let go" as you did when playing Tug.

4. Once your dog is good at bringing the ball back to you from a couple of feet, gradually start to throw the ball farther. With your good play habits established, she should now be eager to get the ball back to you for the continuation of the game. But if at any point she doesn't bring the ball back, either stop the game or run away from her. Next time you throw the ball, make it a

much shorter distance and gradually build up the distance from scratch. Learning to cooperate with Fetch not only strengthens the good habits you established with Tug, it builds up a terrific come-when-called!

"Time Out"

If your play is a bit too intense, a Tug game might get your dog overly excited, which can lead to jumping, mouthiness, and rough behavior. By saying "Okay" and "Let go" frequently in your play sessions, you can often control the level of excitement. But sometimes things can still get too rough. For these occasions, use a "Time Out." If your puppy or dog puts her mouth on you or jumps on you, make a high-pitched "Yipe," a loud "Owwwww," or a low-pitched "Ahhh." I recommend some people use a whistle which can be hung around the neck. The goal is to get her to stop jumping or mouthing you, even for a moment. See which sound works best for your dog. Stop playing for a few seconds. Then, as long as your dog is patiently waiting for the toy, resume the game with an "Okay." If she mouths you or jumps on you again during the play session, declare "Time Out," and put the toy away. Do not resume playing again for at least a few minutes.

By introducing Time Out into your play sessions, you have taught your puppy or dog to respect certain physical boundaries. This will help communicate to her that it is unacceptable to jump on or to put her mouth on human beings. Once your dog has learned "Okay" and "Let go" on a reliable basis and is responding to your requests at least eight times out of ten, Time Out can be used to maintain those good habits. If your dog grabs a toy out of your hand without permission, for example, now you can say "Time Out," stop playing, and put the toy away. You can do the same if your dog does not give you back the toy on request, or if she puts her mouth on your hand. With good habits, your dog will learn to control the excitement herself. She wants the fun to continue, so she will learn to avoid the Time Out by playing in a more cooperative way.

If Your Puppy or Dog Gets Even More Excited...

Some dogs get even more excited when you make the high-pitched "Yipe" or "Owwwww" as you attempt to get her to stop the jumping or mouthing. If this is the case with your dog, skip this vocal interruption and go directly to the Time Out.

Part 3

Integrating Habits to Get Reliable Behavior

Chapter 8

Incorporating Habit Training into Daily Life

Welcome home!

Once your 7-Day Canine Vacation is over, you'll have at least a grade-school equivalency of dogspeak. Now it's time to incorporate habit training into everyday life. As previously stated, it often takes only twenty-one to twenty-eight days to form a new habit. You've already spent a week setting up a great learning environment. And, by playing the magnet game, your dog has learned how rewarding it is to sit, lie down, go-to-his-bed, look to you for direction, and bring you a toy. A solid new habit-forming foundation has been formed so that "good" behaviors become automatic and "bad" habits fade away. The next step to simplify all this has to do with motivating both you and your dog. This is easily accomplished by rewarding a habit with a habit. This brings us to the Premack Principle.

The Premack Principle

The Premack Principle is all about using a high-probability, strong behavior to reinforce a low-probability weaker behavior. This principle was developed by David Premack, hence the name. Let's say you want your puppy or dog to walk by your side in heel position. Your dog, on the other hand, really wants to sniff the fire hydrant. In order to get your dog to really want to stay by your side in heel position, you reward him for heeling by letting him sniff the hydrant. That is, after he's walked by your side for a few steps, you then release him and let him do that he really wants to do. By fulfilling his desire to sniff the hydrant, you've strengthened heeling, a behavior which, from your dog's point of view, is less desirable.

Here's another example: Your dog wants to go outside but acts like a pogo stick and jumps all over you whenever you pick up the leash. Let's say that you put the leash down every time she jumps, and pick it up again whenever she sits. Within a very short period of time, she will learn that the only way she is going to get to go outside—which she really wants to do—is when she is quiet and in a sitting position—something not quite so motivating. The idea is that she only gets what she wants when you get what you want first.

We humans use this principle every day. We tell our children to eat their vegetables before they get ice cream. Or, "Clean your room and then you can use the car." For me, this chapter was really exciting to write. But I also had a deadline for an article for a dog magazine, which wasn't quite as motivating for me as a writer. So I made a deal with myself. If I wrote for an hour on the article, I could write several hours on this chapter. Of course, once I started writing the article I spent more than an hour and actually finished it. That often happens with this technique; you end up getting a lot of stuff done.

The concept of controlling your dog's freedom and access to what she wants and then requiring her to do something before you give it to her seems pretty simple. So what's the problem in just following through and doing that? Us. We're often simply not motivated enough to do it. This brings us to human motivation.

Models for New Habits

Leo Tolstoy said, "Everyone thinks of changing the world, but no one thinks of changing himself." What a great quote. For the purpose of this book, it's all about changing our own habits so our dogs can change their habits. And that's exactly what's happened over the past seven days with the Canine Vacation. A foundation of new habits has been formed that will automatically solve problems so both you and your dog can live happily ever after. In this chapter, we will build on that foundation. Luckily, one or two good habits can solve more than one problem behavior. For example, the good habits of using prevention and playing the magnet game can solve a number of problems, such as jumping, bolting out the door, begging, housetraining, and stealing.

Below you'll find a list of problem behaviors along with the good habits that will solve them. Next to each of the habits, you'll see little boxes. Check off the ones that you'd like to use and see what happens in twenty-eight days. All habits are formed by successful repetitions. To strengthen and burnish them, the repetitions need to be acted out in different situations. For example, just because your dog automatically sits at the front door, you still have to form the "sit" habit at the back door. Once you've done this in several locations, then, no matter where you are or what you're doing, your dog will automatically sit at any door.

> Your own good habits will directly shape your dog's good habits. If you simply form the good habits of prevention along with playing the magnet game to reward behaviors such as sit, down, and going to your bed, these behaviors will soon become your dog's good habits.

All strategies dealing with behavior problems have two components—one component is *prevention*, that is, setting up the environment so the behavior cannot happen and another is *what-to-do*, that is, teaching a good habit that is incompatible with the bad habit. In most cases, *what-to-do* is handled by using the magnet game. For example, if a dog has the bad habit of bolting out the door, you'd first use a tether to prevent that from happening and, second, teach your dog to form the good habit of siting or lying down instead. To get your dog to be more and more reliable at the behaviors *you want*, simply continue to form new habits and then progressively incorporate them in more challenging situations. That is, you'll be gradually adding the 3D's—a greater length of time (***duration***), greater ***distance***, and additional ***distractions***.

The important thing is to make forming the habits fun for you, and your dog, and that you take it at a pace that works for both of you.

Begging

❏ Make a habit of tethering your dog before you sit at the table to eat. (See page 40; also watch online video seminar at *www.DogWhispererDVD.com/habits.*)

❏ Make a habit of teaching your dog to "go to your spot" whenever you eat. (See "Go to Your Spot," page 190; also watch online video seminar at *www.Dog WhispererDVD.com/habits.*)

❏ Make a habit of petting and praising your dog whenever he sits without being asked.

❏ Make a habit of petting and praising your dog whenever he lies down without being asked.

❏ Make a habit of petting and praising your dog whenever he goes to his bed without being asked.

Figure 8-1

Make a habit of teaching your dog to "go to your spot" whenever you eat.

Bolting on Walks

- ❏ Make a habit of putting treats in a pack and always taking them on walks.
- ❏ Make a habit of attaching a water bottle and poop bags to your leash.
- ❏ Make a habit to check your dog's collar before attaching his leash to make sure it's not too loose, which might allow him to slip out of it.
- ❏ Make a habit of putting the leash around your wrist to secure it so it can't be pulled free, instead of holding it in your hand.
- ❏ Make a habit of checking to see if the pavement is too hot for your dog's paws when going on a walk in hot weather by putting your hand on the pavement. If it's too hot for your hand, it's too hot for the paws. (When you're at the beach, check the heat of the sand this way too.)
- ❏ Make a habit of stepping on your dog's leash whenever you stop to talk to someone on your walk.
- ❏ Make a habit of having your dog sit whenever you come to the street corner.
- ❏ Make a habit of always saying "Okay" to release your dog before stepping off the curb.
- ❏ Make a habit of always having your dog in "heel" position when crossing a street.

Figure 8-2

Make a habit of stepping on your dog's leash whenever you stop to talk to someone on your walk.

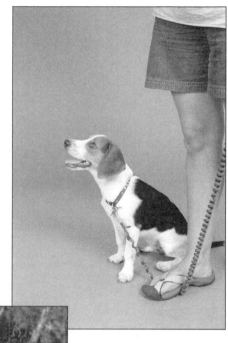

Figure 8-3

Make a habit of having your dog sit whenever you come to the street corner.

Bolting Out the Door or Gate

❑ Make a habit of turning around to see where your dog is and, if necessary, tether or confine him before opening the door.

❑ Make a habit of having your dog sit and stay until you release her when opening the door.

Figure 8-4

Make a habit of having your dog sit and stay until you release her when going out the door.

Car Safety

❏ Make a habit of having your dog sit before he gets in the car.

❏ Make a habit of buckling your dog's seat belt.

❏ Make a habit of having the windows up so that your dog cannot stick his head out.

❏ Make a habit of having your dog sit and stay until you release him out the door.

❏ Make a habit of having your dog sit and stay as soon as he steps out of the car.

Figure 8-5

Make a habit of buckling your dog's
seat belt.

Chewing Inappropriate Objects (slippers, furniture, TV remote, tissue paper, etc.)

- ❏ Make a habit to tether your dog so he can't reach inappropriate objects.
- ❏ Make a habit of giving your dog a Bully stick or a treat-filled Kong whenever he's tethered.
- ❏ Make a habit of policing the area and moving all inappropriate objects out of your dog's reach.
- ❏ Make a habit of having your dog "leave it" (see how to teach leave it on page 200).
- ❏ Make a habit of having your dog "drop it" (see how to teach drop it on page 105).

Figure 8-6

Make a habit of having your dog "leave it."

Digging

- ❏ Make a habit of keeping your dog inside the house or his dog run until you know he won't dig.
- ❏ Make a habit of providing lots of exercise and play so your dog has less energy to dig.

❏ Make a habit of playing Find It #2. (See page 93; also watch online video seminar at *www.DogWhisperer DVD.com/habits*.)

❏ Make a habit of giving your dog appropriate and interesting things to chew on to keep him busy so he doesn't dig.

Figure 8-7

If your dog digs, make a habit of providing lots of exercise and play so your dog has less energy to dig.

Feeding Problems (Jumping and grabbing for food while you're preparing meals)

(Note: Aggression around food is a sign that you need help from a skilled professional trainer. Make sure the one you select uses only positive methods.)

❏ Make a habit of tethering your dog before feeding.
❏ Make a habit of having your dog sit and stay before you release him to eat.
❏ Make a habit of teaching "leave it."

Figure 8-8

Make a habit of tethering your dog
before feeding.

Jumping

❑ Make a habit of tethering your dog before he jumps.

❑ Make a habit of stepping on your dog's leash before he jumps.

❑ Make a habit of putting your hands on your chest and turning your side to the dog if he jumps.

❑ Make a habit of offering low-key greetings when you arrive home.

❑ Make a habit of petting and praising your dog whenever he sits without being asked.

❑ Make a habit of petting and praising your dog whenever he lies down without being asked.

❑ Make a habit of petting and praising your dog whenever he goes to his bed without being asked.

❑ Make a habit of playing Find It #1 before your dog can jump. (See page 85; also watch online video seminar at *www.DogWhispererDVD.com/habits*.)

Figure 8-9

Make a habit of putting your hands on
your chest and turning to your side if
your dog jumps.

House Safety

❏ Make a habit to puppy-proof the house before leaving. This means picking up toys, slippers, and anything else a puppy or new rescue dog can destroy or harm. It also means making a habit to check the locks on the baby gates and crates.

❏ Make a habit of tethering your dog at appropriate times.

Housetraining Problems

❑ Make a habit of taking your dog out after eating, sleeping, and activites.

❑ Make a habit of following a schedule.

❑ Make a habit of using the same word associated with elimination such as hurry up, go potty, go outside, etc.

❑ Make a habit of tethering and crating your dog until the problem is solved.

Stealing

❑ Make a habit of tethering your dog before you sit at the table to eat. (See page 40; also watch online video seminar at *www.DogWhispererDVD.com/habits*.)

❑ Make a habit of policing the house and putting all forbidden objects out of reach.

❑ Make a habit of giving your dog appropriate and interesting things to chew on.

❑ Make a habit of playing Find It #2. (See page 93; also watch online video seminar at *www.DogWhisperer DVD.com/habits*.)

Yard Safety

❑ Make a habit of policing the yard and making sure there are no avenues of escape. This means checking the walls and fencing for breaches, if necessary.

❑ Make a habit of policing the yard and putting all forbidden objects out of reach.

❑ Make a habit of never putting your dog in the yard unsupervised until he is reliable.

❑ Make a habit of giving your dog appropriate and interesting things to chew on such as Bully sticks, treat-filled Kongs, and chicken breast strips.

❑ Make a habit of playing the Find It #2, Tug, and Fetch games. (See Chapter 7.)

Linking New, Desired Habits with Old, Established Habits

The key to making the habit-forming process so easy is to link your new, desired habit with an old, established habit. As an example, I went on a program to improve my health by establishing new exercise habits. The way I did that was to link the new habit of daily exercise with the established habit of making dinner. For example, if I was making soup, every time I got up to stir it, I did a couple of exercises. Within twenty-eight days, the habit was established and now I automatically do a couple of exercises just before I walk into the kitchen. It's a good habit that I'm going to keep.

Here are a few daily examples to consider:

🦴 If you want to teach your dog to sit and stay instead of bolting out the door, use your own mealtime as a mental trigger to do some training. Just before you sit down to eat, take your dog to the door and practice having him sit/stay every time you put your hand on the doorknob. Repeat five to ten times. Reward with treats each time he is successful. Within twenty-eight days he will automatically sit whenever you put your hand on the doorknob. Other daily habits you can link this new habit include whenever you pick up your car keys, whenever you turn the TV on, whenever you finish reading a chapter in a book, or just before you open a newspaper.

☞ If you want your dog to run to his bed instead of begging at the table, ask your dog to go to his bed whenever you sit at the table or sit at the computer. Just before you sit in your chair, ask your dog to go to his bed and reward him. Repeat three times. Within twenty-eight days your dog will automatically run to his bed whenever you sit at the table to eat or sit at the computer to work.

☞ If you have a baby, ask your dog to lie down or go to his bed just before you feed the baby. Reward him and repeat this action three times before every feeding. Within twenty-eight days, your dog will automatically lie down or go to his bed whenever you feed your baby.

For all of these exercises, as time goes by, you would simply add more challenges by adding more time to the behavior, more distance, or more distractions. Within a very short time, your dog will do all the things you ask automatically, including staying in whatever location you asked him to go for as long as you want.

Using Habit Training in Other Areas of Your Life

These same habit-training strategies and methods you are using with your dog can also be used for anything else in your everyday life to achieve what you're looking for. Simply follow the formula. Most people are goal oriented. And if we can see the light at the end of the tunnel, we're more likely to soldier on and persevere until we actually reach our destination. So if we believe that a goal can be reached in a set period of time, like twenty-eight days, most of us are much more willing to give it a shot. Once again, that's the message of this book. Treat your dog the same way that you would treat yourself.

Chapter 9

Motivation

Learning how to fix a puppy or dog's problem behavior is one thing; getting motivated to fix it is another kettle of fish. Millions of puppies and dogs are euthanized in shelters each year because of problems like biting, jumping, chewing, digging, etc. To a large extent, it all comes down to a lack of training. Some people don't know how to train their dogs, but others simply aren't motivated to do so. This chapter directly addresses the motivation issue. In the next chapter, I'll address willpower, which is another vital part of the equation. Motivation triggers our efforts to do something and willpower charges and fuels those efforts until the goal is reached.

This book is unique because it not only offers specific step-by-step instructions on how to get your dog motivated to do what you want him to do, it also includes step-by-step instructions on how to get *you* motivated to actually do the training. The fact that you're reading this book is a great indication that you are strongly motivated. That being said, this chapter does include some unique tips that you might find interesting. But if you want, you can just skip it and move on.

No goal, whether it be in dog training, finances, physical health, acting, dancing with the stars, construction, or personal relationships can be achieved without strong motivation and a powerful will. Can't happen. Never will. In a nutshell, success depends on know-how mixed with desire, conviction, and perseverance. Even if we know what to do, we still have to be motivated to do it. If you have a hammer but you're never motivated to pick it up and pound a nail with it, the hammer itself is useless. If you collect recipes but are never motivated to cook, the recipes are only pipe dreams of scrumptious foods that you never actually get to taste. If you've read dog training books and watched dog training DVDs but don't use the tools you've been given, your dog's problem behaviors will never be resolved. It isn't just about knowing what to do, we have to *want* to use and apply that knowledge.

Human Motivation, Starting with Mother Nature and All She's Worth

Think of the big outdoors. Soft breezes, warm temperatures, swaying trees, peaceful animals, the gently lapping waves of the deep blue ocean . . . ahhhh! Mother Nature at her finest. Her majestic beauty and awesome marvels help us relax, inspire us, and soothe our troubles away. But she can also destroy any semblance of you or your dog's self-control.

If Mother Nature wafts the smell of a dog in heat by your dog's nose, or struts a squirrel in his path, or beckons him to respond to the howls of a neighbor dog's greeting, who's worth more? You, shouting, "Here, boy!"—or the chattering, fluffy-tailed squirrel? Competing with Mother Nature is not something many of us are motivated to do.

> Finding your motivation is the first step to motivating your dog.

Motivating a dog to listen to you when the sights, sounds, and smells of the world smother his senses can be a lot of work. The key to successfully motivating your dog to pay more attention to you than to all Mother Nature has to offer is to first learn how to motivate yourself.

But the truth is, most people simply aren't all that motivated to do anything about a problem behavior unless the neighbors are complaining, the house is being torn up, or someone's getting hurt.

If a dog's incessant barking has been going on for years, chances are the person learned to simply tune it out. Even if a dog is causing problems as a self-employed home decorator, gardener, or neighborhood alarm system, many people simply avoid taking the time and spending the energy to train him because they're exhausted from a hard day's work or there's something better to do like eat, read the paper, watch television, or take a nap.

Connecting the Dots

Everything I'm saying here about getting-motivated-to-get-motivated has been written before but never in a dog training book. As a result of this omission, many people have come to believe that dog training is some mysterious process, with unknown secret procedures and methods. But motivating and educating the family dog uses the same psychology used to reach any other goal in life. That's the message—use the same methods with your dog that you are already using in everyday life. The problem is many people rarely are able to "connect the dots" between "dog" psychology and human psychology. Really, there's no difference.

My brother Tom and his wife Kathy were visiting old friends. As they sat down to reminisce, my brother's friend put his two Golden Retrievers in the basement so they "couldn't jump on people and bother them." He didn't know what else to do. If my brother's friend was talking about his children, he would know what to do. But he couldn't see the similarities between the psychology he uses with his children and the methods used with his dogs. To a great extent, parenting is parenting. A couple of months later my brother called his friend to see how things were going and learned that he had given the dog away.

In my first book, *The Dog Whisperer*, I related the story of the psychiatrist wife and psychologist husband who called me for help because they, like my brother's friend, also kept their dog in the basement due to jumping problems. These two professionals knew more about psychology and classical and operant conditioning than I ever knew or will know. But, just like my brother's friend, they just never applied what they knew to their dog. They, too, never connected the dots.

How to Get Yourself Motivated: The Art of Picturing the Future

Millions of dollars are spent each year in the motivation industry. Anthony Robbins, Deepak Chopra, Colin Powell, and every participant who ever appeared on The Biggest Loser weight-loss reality TV show makes money teaching people how to get motivated. Well, now you're reading a book about dog training. Finally you've found the best source of motivational training ever!

The message from all these self-help gurus and life coaches is to first believe that we can attain whatever we want in life. In other words, if we picture the future we want, it's more likely to happen. With a little hope, curiosity is aroused. With curiosity, motivation is triggered. Add a little know-how, and the impossible often becomes possible. The way to get motivated to do all this is to follow the habit-forming formula we introduced in Chapter 5. To review, the Four Steps for Habit Power are:

Step 1. Identify Your Goal
Step 2. Form a Strategy
Step 3. Implement the Strategy
Step 4. Maintain the New Habit

For dog training purposes, the goal we've identified is: Get motivated to train. What about Step 2, strategy? As we discussed in Chapter 5, a strategy means identifying the habits that will lead toward the goal. So what habits will lead to that goal? Here is a list to consider:

Seven Habits to Get You Motivated

Throughout my thirty-five-year career, teaching tens of thousands of people how to train their dogs, I found that those who were most successful in training were those with the most passion. That's where my second profession, as a yoga and stress management instructor, really came in handy. I came up with the seven most powerful habits that can help anyone get passionate, especially when it comes to training their dog.

These seven habits are geared to keep you motivated by keeping you calm and focused. This, in turn, keeps your dog more focused on you—and you both become more motivated to continue. So I suggest experimenting with three or four or even five of the habits listed below over the next twenty-eight days and see what happens.

1. Breathe
2. Eat Something
3. Be Quiet
4. Talk to Yourself
5. Move
6. The Clothes Connection
7. Create a Support System

Habit #1: Breathe

Is your breathing deep and controlled or is it shallow? *How* we breathe positively or negatively affects how motivated we are to do anything. Motivation is actually just thought and action that we've harnessed.

Why it works: Deep breathing changes the blood chemistry by oxygenating the blood and releasing endorphins. In short, breathing influences thought, which influences how we feel, which influences how we act. Control the breath, control the behavior.

What to do: Do a couple of complete breaths, as described in the following section, before every training session.

The Complete Breath Exercise

The complete breath consists of a smooth inhalation and then a smooth exhalation through the nose for equal amounts of time. (This exercise is also referred to as the relaxation breath or diaphragmatic breathing.) Some people aren't used to having their lungs full of air so if you feel lightheaded or dizzy, stop and take a break. Wait a few minutes and then do one complete breath instead of a series of breaths.

1. Do this exercise with your eyes closed or open. Either way, you'll benefit from this exercise but you'll be able to concentrate a little better with your eyes closed.

2. Now imagine your lungs divided into three parts: top, middle, and lower. Be sure that your mouth is closed and then start to breathe in through your nose. Feel the lower part of the lungs fill up first, and as you

do so, allow the stomach to expand slightly. (If you are used to tightening the stomach muscles inward when you breathe, as many people do, it may take a few practice breaths to reverse this process so you will receive the full benefits of the breath.) Then, when the lower part of your lungs feel full, allow the oxygen to fill the middle part of the chest. Then fill the top of your lungs. Once you have inhaled completely, your chest will have expanded and your shoulders will draw upward and backward a bit.

3. Now, without pausing, begin a smooth exhalation, again through your nose. Picture your lungs as two slowly deflating balloons as the air is expelled from the top of your lungs and on downward to the bottom. When you are close to the end of the exhalation, gently push your stomach muscles inward and a little upward toward the spine to expel any remaining air in the lungs.

4. Next, immediately after the exhalation, begin a new breath by gently inhaling.

CAUTION: If you feel light-headed or dizzy, stop. The key is to relax, not strain. Experiment with one breath and progress from there gradually.

When you first begin to do this exercise, do a round of three complete breaths, timing your inhalation and exhalation so they are equal in length. A good starting place is a count of three or four on the inhalation and a count of three or four on the exhalation. The goal is to move slowly and smoothly—completely exhaling one breath before inhaling the next breath.

When I gave up smoking many years ago, every time I caught myself thinking about lighting up, I would focus on this breathing exercise. Over time, it became a habit and I no longer had to think about doing it. The complete breath was automatically triggered every time I had an impulse to smoke and gradually the impulse to smoke was replaced by breathing. You can see how something as simple as remembering to breathe can be used as a powerful substitute behavior (habit) to solve any number of dog-related issues, as well as any of your own destructive habits or thoughts. The bottom line is that your thoughts and your actions are impacted by breath; and hence breath affects everything you do. (For more on Breathing, view the online video seminar at *www.Dog WhispererDVD.com/habits.*)

Habit #2: Eat Something

Without fuel our internal engine slows. Get in the habit of eating good fuel and your mind and body will feel like doing something.

Why it works: Proteins, carbohydrates, and fats are metabolized to create energy that fuels our bodies. Food affects how we feel, what we think, and what we do.

What to do: If you're not feeling like getting up off the chair to walk your dog, eat a little something nutritious—put an apple in your mouth, eat a banana, or chew some string cheese. Nutritious food keeps us healthy and helps us focus and concentrate.

Habit #3: Be Quiet

No matter how powerful any self-help dog training program is, mental chatter can sabotage even the most sincere efforts to succeed. By mental chatter, I'm referring to any and all unconscious conversation that does not promote your goals. In other words, if your goal is to become healthy, wealthy, and wise, sniping, griping, complaining, and worrying does nothing to foster those goals. A critically important aspect of changing the way you think and behave is to get in the habit of hearing your own inner dialogue. On a conscious level, most people are unaware of incessant self-talk. Once you have learned to "listen" to what's going on in your head, you can take the reins and replace idle chatter with constructive thoughts.

Why it works: By becoming aware of trivial thoughts and replacing them with positive and constructive thoughts, time is no longer wasted and goals become reality much sooner. Doing so will allow you to focus on dog training—or anything else in life—with focus and conviction.

What to do: Whenever you become aware that you're in the middle of unconstructive mental chatter, like blaming your dog for eliminating in the house, destroying the furniture, or digging up the garden, take a couple of controlled breaths. The more you do this, the less complaining you'll do and your controlled breathing will automatically trigger whenever that negativity begins to chatter away.

Habit #4: Talk to Yourself

Anyone over forty is going to love this one. To help form any new habit, sometimes you'll need a reminder to do what you're supposed to be doing. By constantly reminding yourself, either mentally or out loud, to do something, your body will start to listen to you and respond more and more quickly. Reminding yourself out loud is particularly helpful. When we say anything out loud, a part of the brain is activated that is different from our thoughts alone. For example, if you take your umbrella into the movie theater, as you walk into the theater turn to your friend and say, "I'm going to remember to pick up this umbrella when we leave." (Whether stated out loud or internally, be sure you use only positive, affirmative statements.) But, if you talk to yourself out loud when you're alone, I might recommend you wear a phone headset so your blabbing doesn't look too weird as you walk along the street. And maybe it's not a good thing to do in elevators.

Why it works: Talking to yourself allows you to see how you feel about something. You can look at things from a different perspective. Here's where we distinguish the inner dialogue of negative self-talk in tip number three, Being Quiet, with positive dialogue that you are directing. In other words, you are in control of the chatter. Conscious chatter is strengthening. Unconscious mental chatter is weakening; As an example, you'll often hear professional athletes shout "let's go!" or some other phrase after a missed shot to help motivate themselves to concentrate more and try harder.

What to do: If you are forming the habit of stepping on your dog's leash so your dog will automatically sit instead of jump on people, remind yourself, "Step on the leash" over and over.

Habit #5: Move

Lethargy begets couch potato-itis. The trick to getting motivated to do everyday things like walking and exercise, washing the car, cleaning the house, or playing with your dog is to start with a small victory and build up to the bigger ones. The small victory is creating a habit of moving your body. Even simple exercises or body movements will be energizing.

Why it works: Any time you decide to move your body, you are initiating an act of will, which opens the door to the vault of past physical experiences. These are memories of actions which resulted in you successfully reaching a goal, which will then trigger the physiological responses (adrenaline, endorphins, etc.) associated with those experiences. In other words, you'll feel better.

What to do: The simple act of clenching and relaxing your fists and tightening and relaxing areas of your body is an act of will. When you combine controlled breathing with body tensing exercises, it's like calling on all your reserves to help you out. You become a mighty army of one, ready to GET UP AND MOVE! The next time lethargy sets in and you're not motivated to play with your dog, try this experiment: clench both fists and then release them. Do it three times. Now clench your fists, and, at the same time, tighten your arms, chest, and face. Repeat this three times. These simple exercises can be used to motivate you to act and get up and walk your dog.

Habit #6: The Clothes Connection

"Clothes make the man (and woman!)." Every morning I've made it a habit to walk a mile to my favorite coffee shop where I read the paper, munch on a bagel, and sip my coffee. On the mornings when I'm not too thrilled about taking the walk, and think about skipping a day, I make it a point to automatically reach for my jacket. Change your clothes (even in your imagination); change the way you feel.

Why it works: Clothes become a touchstone for motivation. By consistently wearing the same clothes while connected with any given activity, the clothes become synonymous with that activity. So by grabbing my jacket, I trigger my motivation to walk and short-circuit the thought of staying home. In this case, my jacket has become a touchstone for taking the walk.

What to do: If you're a dance instructor and not too thrilled about teaching a specific class, grab your dancing shoes. Running shoes motivate exercise, a party dress motivates dancing, a football jersey triggers partying on Sunday afternoon, and so on. One more thing. Your touchstone doesn't have to be clothes. If you're not too thrilled about walking your dog, just get up and grab the leash and you'll probably notice right away that you feel more motivated to go on a walk.

Habit #7: Create a Support System

Why are there so many gyms, support groups for dieting, and group dog training classes available? We're a social species.

Why it works: We gather strength and emotional support from people around us. They motivate us. Whether training your dog, dieting, or exercising, doing any of these things with a friend makes it all easier. It isn't a necessity but disciplining yourself seems to be easier when you're with others who are doing the same thing.

What to do: Get a dog-walking group of friends together and walk your dogs at specific times during the day. Even when you are less inclined to walk, the thought of not joining the group on the walk will motivate you to do it anyway. Create a habit of reaching out to others and, over time, establish a strong social network. One way to do this is to go online to *www.MeetUp.com* and find a group in your area on a topic that interests you, such as dogs. Whenever a sabotaging thought of lethargy hits you, call someone. If walking your dog is a daily habit you're trying to form and you don't feel like walking, call a friend or a couple of friends and form a walking group. I see gangs of mothers walking with their baby strollers all the time.

Motivation as a New Habit

Here's an example of how the Four Steps for Habit Power looks with motivation to train your dog as the goal:

Step 1: Identify the Goal:
🦴 Get motivated to train my dog

Step 2: Form a Strategy:
🦴 Choose one or more of the following habits:

- Breathe
- Eat
- Be Quiet
- Talk to Yourself
- Move
- Get Dressed
- Create a Support System

Step 3: Implement the Strategy
🦴 Do the things you've checked off

Step 4: Maintain the New Habit

Let's say you've checked off breathing as one of the habits that you'll be forming to help motivate yourself. Whenever the weak thought of not wanting to walk your dog presents itself, you will consciously take three breaths and go about your day. Within twenty-eight days of committing to this new habit and following these steps, you'll find yourself automatically start to breathe whenever the thought of not wanting to walk your dog presents itself. As the days go by, you'll find that it presents itself less and less. So whenever the thought of "I should walk my dog but I don't feel like it" strikes, you will see that your breathing will begin to trigger automatically. The breathing will trigger your endorphins, which are relaxing and stress relieving. This opens the door to feeling good about walking your dog. Once you feel good about walking your dog, you can now you can use the same formula over the next twenty-eight days to form a daily habit of actually walking your dog and teaching him not to pull you down the street. Once those twenty-eight days have gone by, it'll all be automatic.

Dog Motivation

Now let's look at motivating dogs. Motivation is based on desire and the anticipation of the fulfillment of that desire. You and your dog can be motivated with positives or negatives. It's the old "carrot or stick" analogy. You can motivate your dog to stop doing something by hitting him with a "stick" through the use of aversive methods such as hitting, jerking on a leash, pinning, shocking, making intimidating sounds like growling or "shushing," or other acts of intimidation or the use of physical force. Or you can motivate him to do what you want him to do instead by using "carrots," that is petting, praise, treats, and other positive rewards. Obviously this book is about using positive methods.

Over the years, behavioral scientists have found that aversive training methods, which are erroneously based on the simplistic and outdated concept of alpha dominance, can provoke fearful or defensively aggressive behavior.

In a recent article in ScienceDaily, *If You're Aggressive, Your Dog Will Be Too Says Veterinary Study*, Meghan E. Herron spoke about her study of confrontational or aversive dog training methods at the University of Pennsylvania. Herron said, "Our study demonstrated that many confrontational training methods, whether staring down dogs, striking them, or intimidating them with physical manipulation does little to correct improper behavior and can elicit aggressive responses."

The Six Most Common Negative Training Methods

The six most commonly used aversive training methods are poking (jabbing), pinning to the ground, hanging by the leash, shocking, leash corrections using choke and prong collars, and physically forcing dogs into situations they are afraid of. These methods are used by some trainers to motivate dogs to stop doing unacceptable behaviors and they are occasionally effective. But they aren't kind and they aren't necessary. Obviously, I do not promote nor do I condone such methods.

In the study, which was published by *Applied Animal Behavior Science*, Herron and her coauthors say this about confrontational training methods: "Their common use may have grown from the premise that canine misbehavior or aggression is rooted in social dominance (to the owner), or, conversely, to a lack of assertiveness or dominance by the owner. Advocates of such theories suggest that owners need to establish themselves as the 'alpha' or 'pack leader,' using physical manipulations and intimidation in order to do so, thereby forcing the dog into a subordinate attitude. While the use of confrontational training methods to subdue hypothetical dominance is commonplace, the current scientific literature suggests, instead, that canine aggression and other behavior problems are not a result of dominant behavior or lack of the owner's 'alpha' status, but rather a result of fear (self-defense) or underlying anxiety problems, important for an understanding of the motivation and treatment of aggression."

So what positive motivators will be effective for your dog? It's up to you to know how to motivate and what motivators to use in any given situation. The stuff that motivates your dog is in constant flux owing to her previous life experiences, her emotional state (fear, excitement, stress), her health, her genetic influences (what she was bred to do), how much freedom she has, the time of day, distractions, and so on. (Review Contextual Behaviors on page 13.) The fluctuating values of these motivators directly affect how successful you will be in getting your dog to do what you want her to do. For example, what if your dog just had a full meal? For an hour or so anyway, a piece of chicken or steak may not be as strong a motivator as it otherwise would, while fetching a tennis ball may be a real thrill. What if your dog is frightened by something? Again, food may no longer be a motivator because your dog is concentrating on whether she should fight or run away. If your dog isn't feeling well, even a freshly cooked steak can lose its appeal. And if she's tired, going for a walk may no longer motivate her.

By using this knowledge of fluctuating and differential motivators (one thing being stronger than another), we can actually manufacture and shape our dogs' desires to get them to do what we ask. This brings us to the concept of controlling access to what your dog wants.

Manufactured Motivation

The more you control access to what your dog wants, the more motivated your dog will be to follow your lead and do what you want him to do. For example:

🦴 A hungry dog is more motivated by food. So if you control when he eats and how much he eats throughout the day, he will pay more attention to you than if he is able to eat whenever he wants because food is available all day long.

🦴 A well-exercised dog is more motivated to pay attention to you instead of jumping or running away.

🦴 Freedom is a powerful motivator. A dog who is tethered pays more attention to you because you are the one who controls access to what he wants. In addition, you are the one to reward him just as soon as he does something you want him to do, like sit or lie down. He soon learns what behaviors get him what he wants. For example, if your dog is tethered and somebody walks into the room, your dog can get that person to come up and say hello by lying down. Another example is walking your dog on a leash, which is the same principle as being tethered. In this case, the dog is tethered to you. If your dog does what you ask, you can allow him the freedom to sniff a fire hydrant, greet another dog, chase a ball, say hello to members of the family, eat, go for a walk, go swimming, and so on.

By controlling access to toys, food, and freedom, your dog becomes motivated to "work" for that which he desires and follow your lead. After a period of time, these behaviors become habits and restraint and confinement are no longer necessary.

The Motivation and Rewards Value Triangle on page 155 lists many of the life rewards and food rewards that can be used to motivate your dog. The rewards on the top of the triangle, labeled as "great stuff," are often of much higher value than those at the bottom. *However, it's important to note that these values fluctuate and take on greater or lesser importance as training progresses.* For example, going for a walk or playing Fetch or Tug may leap in value over certain foods. The trick is knowing what will motivate your dog the most at any given time.

A Note About Food Treats

The power of habit training is that once your dog forms a new habit, you rarely have to use treats because your dog has gotten used to paying attention to you as the source of everything he wants and treats are no longer necessary. The reward becomes you and all the wonderful stuff you have to offer, such as the life rewards listed in The Motivation and Rewards Value Triangle.

The value of these rewards and the degree to which your dog will be motivated to attain them is directly related to two things:

Figure 9-1

The Motivation and Rewards Value Triangle

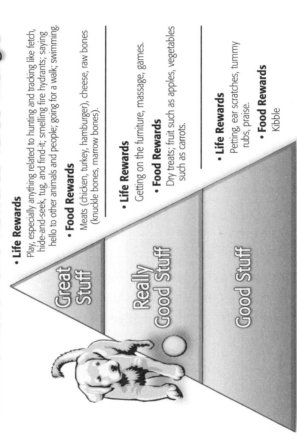

Great Stuff

- **Life Rewards**
  Play, especially anything related to hunting and tracking like fetch, hide-and-seek, tug, and find-it; smelling fire hydrants; saying hello to other animals and people; going for a walk; swimming.
- **Food Rewards**
  Meats (chicken, turkey, hamburger), cheese, raw bones (knuckle bones, marrow bones).

Really Good Stuff

- **Life Rewards**
  Getting on the furniture, massage, games.
- **Food Rewards**
  Dry treats; fruit such as apples, vegetables such as carrots.

Good Stuff

- **Life Rewards**
  Petting, ear scratches, tummy rubs, praise.
- **Food Rewards**
  Kibble

This triangle illustrates the hierarchical values of rewards for most dogs, in most situations, which can be used to reach any goal.

155

1. How much you control access to these things
2. Your attitude (Also see Chapter 4, The Motivating Power of Play)

The concept of controlling your dog's freedom and access to what she wants and then requiring her to do something before you give it to her seems pretty simple. So what's the problem in just following through and doing that? Us. Even if we're motivated, sometimes we simply lose interest and don't follow through. We get distracted whenever life throws obstacles in the way. But distractions come with the territory, so to speak. It seems that as soon as we have decided to finally start a daily routine like walking the dog, playing Fetch, or regular training sessions, all of a sudden we find ourselves doing something else. People we haven't heard from for years suddenly come to visit for a week. Or a family member gets sick. Or a job has a special project with a challenging deadline. All these things can interfere with the schedule you've set for yourself. It's at those times your motivation gets tested and it takes a powerful mental resolve to continue whatever routine you've set up. And that leads us to willpower.

Chapter 10

Willpower

Schools across the country set aside a day each year called Career Day. Professionals from all walks of life are invited to share with the students what they do for a living—and that includes professional dog trainers. I always begin Career Day talks by suggesting to students that they pursue a career that accomplishes three things:

1. Love what you do
2. Contribute to the world in a beneficial way through your work
3. Make money

Then I tell the kids, "No matter what you choose to do for a living, your success is directly linked to your own self-control. Dog trainers have to develop a high degree of self-control to be successful. "After all," I say, "you can't expect a dog to develop self-control if you don't have self-control yourself." Animals respond to what we do and how we act. If we're not calm and relaxed, our dogs won't be calm and relaxed. And if we're not having fun while training our dogs, our dog won't be having fun either.

Developing self-control, of course, requires a high degree of personal willpower, which is needed to be successful in any life's work, whether you are training your dog, selling life insurance, being a parent, or anything else. Roy Baumeister, a psychology professor at Florida State University wrote in *Current Directions in Psychological Science*, "Learning self-control produces a wide range of positive outcomes. Kids do better in school, people do better at work. Look at just about any major category of problem that people are suffering from and odds are pretty good that self-control is implicated in some way. Learning to bring your behavior under control even with arbitrary rules does build character in that it makes you better able to achieve the things you want to achieve later on."

And all this leads us back to the premise of this book. In order to form good habits, a behavior needs to be repeated over and over and this takes willpower. Using habits is the quickest way to be successful and this includes shaping your dog's good habits.

Strengthening Willpower

Raise your arm over your head. That took an act of will. Now do it again and try to keep it there for as long as you can. That

Figure 10-1

The Model for Success

MOTIVATION
leads to practicing self control
which develops willpower
which leads to forming good habits
which leads to success.
YAY!

concentrated effort takes willpower. Now lower your arm. That act also took an act of will. Repeatedly willing your arm to lift and then lower several times in a row not only builds muscle strength, it builds willpower. Just like a muscle, willpower is something that can be strengthened or weakened. In other words, use it or lose it. Every time you mentally or physically exert self-control, it's as if you are putting money in a bank vault. Throughout the day, every little act of self-control and concentrated thought and action contributes to building a powerful will. In this case, instead of saving cash, you are accruing willpower. This willpower energy will grow exponentially. The potential here is for a dramatic effect on the outcome of any situation.

How does this relate to the family dog? Dogs follow leaders. Leadership exudes an attitude of conviction, confidence, and determination. Leadership does not involve physical punishment. This is why positive trainers don't have to resort to hitting, pinning a dog to the ground, using leash corrections, and all the rest. Leadership is fueled by willpower. And willpower is strengthened by self-control.

Strengthening one's willpower is easily accomplished by testing ourselves with little, everyday challenges. With strong willpower, virtually any goal can be reached. Let's say you haven't eaten any dinner and you're hungry. You open the refrigerator door and look at the ice cream (or beer or leftover pizza or chocolate truffles). Then you close the refrigerator. That took willpower. Resisting an impulse to satisfy a bodily urge is self-control. And, once again, self-control builds willpower. Or let's say you hit the snooze button every day of the week so you can catch an extra fifteen minutes of shut-eye. By ignoring that button one day a week—and, instead, getting up and doing fifteen extra minutes of exercise or meditation or prayer, or taking your dog for a walk, or cooking a hot breakfast for the other members of the family, you've strengthened your willpower.

Kathleen Vohs, professor of marketing at the University of Minnesota, says that in lab studies self-control is boosted when people conjure up powerful memories of the things they value in life. Laughter and positive thoughts also help people perform better on self-control tasks. In an interview with the *New York Times,* Dr. Vohs said, "You want to look good in a bikini next summer but you're looking at a piece of chocolate cake now. When we get people to think about values we move them to the long-term state, and that cools off the tempting stimuli."

A Willpower Building Experiment

This book is all about results. If something doesn't work for you, don't continue doing it. With that in mind, here's a willpower building experiment you can try. The theory is that when you practice self-control, you are building an inner reservoir of energy. There's a yoga term for this energy build-up called tapas, which literally means heat or fire. Building up this energy slowly is like building a huge furnace of energy that can be used to fuel your willpower for use whenever you want in attaining your goals. But if you try to do too much new stuff all at once—that is, try to change your life drastically without consideration of what's realistic for you—all of your resolutions can burn up. You'll find yourself feeling resentful, angry, or lethargic—sure signs you've done too much, too soon. Basically this conflict arises out of an emotional and physical taffy-pull between your established, comfortable routines and your new self-control efforts. It's as if you have one nature that says "Gimmee" and another nature that says, "No, do this instead."

The willpower-building experiment that I'm suggesting could be a positive experience for you—or a negative experience. The difference has to do with whether or not you feel free to choose. If you do the experiment and immediately feel resentment, anger, frustration, something's amiss. Obviously something is rubbing you the wrong way. So, if that happens, stop doing it. The idea is to play with this, not compete with it.

The whole purpose of the exercise is to put energy in your inner reservoir, which is done by being positive, not take energy out, which is done by feeling cranky. Keep things in moderation and experiment only with what you feel you can handle.

Below is a selection of everyday activities. Choose one or two that you have confidence that you can complete. The experiment runs for twenty-eight days. Remember, this is simply an experiment—the goal is to make it fun.

Here is what will happen. I guarantee that while you are doing this twenty-eight-day experiment a situation will pop up in your life that requires you to make a decision to do something you won't want to do—something that you would normally put off or do grudgingly. Then you'll think of this willpower experiment. When that happens, you'll automatically tap in to the strength of the willpower that you've accrued in your savings account.

Don't pick more items from the list than you can honestly, realistically complete. And you can't miss a day. If you do, you will you have to start the twenty-eight-day process all over again.

- Pick a meal—breakfast, lunch, or dinner—and limit yourself to ten mouthfuls of food. (Keep all other daily eating habits the same.)
- Every day, before you get out of bed, lie flat on your back and do three complete breaths.
- Every night, before you roll over to fall asleep, do three complete breaths.
- Before every meal or snack, do three complete breaths.
- Before every meal that you eat at home, walk your dog around the block. While on your walk, do three complete breaths.
- Before every meal, do ten bicep curls (lifts) with ten pound weights. (Use a lighter weight if that is appropriate for you.)
- Do something with or for someone else at a certain time each day, such as a phone call, an e-mail, a lunch date, or a gift of a flower.

Obviously, this experiment is about building willpower. If it isn't your cup of tea, just skip it. You'll still benefit from everything else in this book. If you decide to do the will-power experiment above, it's important you complete all twenty-eight days. When it comes to developing a powerful will, it's imperative that you follow through with any resolution you make. So, whatever you choose to do, make sure that it's realistic; otherwise you'll actually weaken your willpower instead of strengthening it.

Set Points

The self-help methods presented in this book may ring a note of familiarity to those readers who have studied any of the world's many self-help philosophies. It's a simple message: We are where we are physically, emotionally, financially, and behaviorally because, essentially, we put ourselves there. That's a very empowering concept because it means we can put ourselves somewhere else. Bad habits can be replaced with good habits. Because this is a book about dog behavior, applying this concept means our good habits can change our dog's unwanted habits to desirable habits. This all might make more sense if we look at the ancient idea of set points.

According to the theory of set points, each of us has a physical, emotional, and biological comfort zone. It's like a preferred maintenance zone of well-being where we feel "in control." Our exercise habits, eating habits, communication style, daily routine, body weight, responses to stress, and so on are all set by us like a thermostat—our own mental, physical, emotional thermostat. Let's say you've been overweight for five or ten years and decide to lose twenty or thirty or even fifty pounds. You work really hard. It might take a year—but

Ta Da! You did it. But just because you lost the weight does not mean the weight will stay off. If you haven't reset your emotional set point, that is, the feeling associated with the weight, there's a good chance you'll slowly drift back into the bad habits that induced the heavier weight in the first place. People who win the lottery get a tremendous kick of joy and relief. But there are many stories of people with huge lottery wins who ended up back where they were before they hit the jackpot. For these people, their emotional set point can't handle the lifestyle wealth provides. One person's set point may be simply to have enough food and water to survive. That is their personal comfort zone of well-being, if only on an unconscious level.

During the course of a lifetime each of us acquires one or more set points, depending on our circumstances. The trick is to learn to become aware of our set points and then choose to either accept them or change them. If we don't, then it's like we become puppets to our own circumstances and stay on the same merry-go-round without improving our circumstances.

If you've become comfortable with—or stopped notic-ing—your dog's undesirable behavior, your physical and emotional set points both have to change. Once again, as often repeated throughout this book, this simply means your own habits have to change. Once your habits change, it's simply a matter of effortless management; that is, monitoring yourself so the new habits can "harden" like cement hardens to form a solid foundation.

This entire book is rooted in twenty-eight-day experi-ments. See what happens and go from there.

By using the tools of motivation and willpower, virtually any behavior can be made into a habit and, as a result, any goal can be attained and any problem solved. This will be great news to your dog who was wondering when you were going to figure this out.

The neat thing about habits is this: Even if you stop doing the behavior, such as when you go on vacation, it will still easily come back to you when you saddle up again. This is true even for habits that you stop doing for years and then resume. Musicians and athletes are among those who often have first-hand knowledge of the power of old habits that have been dormant and then are easily reclaimed when they once again plunge into a specific activity. Unfortunately, the reverse also holds true. Bad habits can resurface if a substitute good habit hasn't had a chance to "ripen." If you have a bad habit—smoking, lying, overeating or drinking, allowing your dog to jump on the table—it's important to stay in a no-temptation environment while the new habit becomes solidly entrenched.

Chapter 11

Basic Behaviors: Pay Attention, Sit, Down, Stay, Come, Go-to-Your-Spot, Leave It, and Heel

Once you and your dog have completed the 7-Day Vacation for Canine Education, you're ready to start teaching specific behaviors. By focusing on "Taking Photos" (also known as the Magnet Game) and playing games during the 7-day vacation, you have heightened your ability to communicate with your dog and created a superhighway in the training process. (Note: If you did not yet take the 7-day vacation, please read Chapters 6 and 7 again and go "on vacation" before you continue on. If necessary, review "Take Photos" on page 75 and "Games to Play on Vacation," Chapter 7.)

Your dog is now able to understand what you want much more quickly; you have a working knowledge of a new language—"dogspeak." From this point forward, all of your dog training will be faster, easier, and more effective. Now you are ready to train your dog for specific behaviors. The training methods for specific behaviors in this chapter are the same methods I've taught for decades and in my DVDs and previous books. The only difference is that you and your dog will proceed at a faster pace and have a great deal more fun doing it.

The behaviors presented in this chapter are all the basics: pay attention, sit, lie down, stay, come, go-to-your-spot, leave it, and heel. Once your dog is successful with any one of these behaviors in a nondistracting environment, you will add the 3D's to get your dog reliable—duration (length of time), distance, and distractions.

All behaviors are taught using my three-step method, preceded by preparation:

Preparation for Training:

- Don't feed your dog before the lessons.
- Use treats that your puppy and dog will highly value, such as small pieces of roast turkey, chicken, hamburger, or cheese. Even if your dog loves his regular dog treats, they are probably not enticing enough for the training process. This is the time to bring out special treats that can compete with distractions and get his attention. Be sure to use small pieces so your dog doesn't become disinterested in the training process because she's so full of treats.
- Keep the treats handy; a treat pouch around your waist is suggested for fast and easy retrieval.

🦴 Start each behavior in "starting position," with your hands on your chest. Since dogs focus on movement, this position will limit any extraneous hand motions that could confuse him.

If You Have More Than One Dog in the Home

The key to using habit training in a multiple dog household has to do with prevention and individualization. If you have two dogs, it's really like you have three dogs. One dog has to be trained individually, then the other, then both together. But it's easier than it sounds.

For example, by tethering one dog (prevention) you can then work with your other dog without interruption or dog-to-dog competition. Then you will ask your untethered dog to sit, lie down, leave it, come, etc. At the same time you will play the magnet game with your tethered dog. Every time you see your tethered dog lie down or sit, you throw her some treats. So one dog is being asked to do something and the other is being rewarded for unasked-for behaviors. After a few minutes of this, simply reverse the roles. This is the easiest and quickest way to remove any dog-to-dog competition because dogs learn that by relaxing and being a good audience, treats come their way. They learn they don't have to fight for anything.

Figure 11-1

Start each behavior in "starting position,"
with your hands on your chest.

The Three-Step Training Process

Step 1: Get the behavior. Get the behavior by using a lure while using a hand signal. Once your dog is successful at this level, progress to step 2.

Step 2: Add the word (vocal signal). Use a verbal cue together with a hand signal to elicit the behavior.

Step 3: Use the word (vocal signal) only. Use only the verbal cue without a visual signal to elicit the behavior.

Training Rules

🦴 **Repeat the beheavior.** After each repetition of a behavior, get your dog to move by throwing a treat and saying "Find it." Then repeat the step.

🦴 **The 80-Percent Rule:** Once your dog is reliable with any specific step in a behavior, that is, he'll do it eight out of every ten times you ask, you're ready to increase the challenge.

🦴 **The "3D's":** Always begin the training of any new bchaviui in a nondistracting environment. When your dog meets each step or level of challenge eight out of ten times, you will move on to the next, more challenging step or level by gradually adding:

- **Duration:** First, add longer duration (length of time you're asking your dog to do the behavior);
- **Distance:** Then add greater distance (how far away you are from your dog when asking for the behavior);
- **Distractions:** Finally, you'll add more distractions (getting your dog to keep his attention on you in the midst of more and more sights, sounds, and touch, until he is able to focus on you even when a squirrel is nearby).

🦴 **Return to Step One When the Context Changes:** Whenever you change the training context or environment, such as moving the training session from the kitchen to the living room, the backyard, or the street, always start teaching the behavior from scratch; that is, return to step one for each and every behavior. (See Contextual Behaviors, page 13.)

🦴 **Food Treats and Weaning Off Treats:** At first you will use a food treat as a lure every single time your dog does what you want when training for a specific behavior. Then, as you go through the training process, consistently ask your dog to do more and more with praise as the only reward—using food treats less and less often and then only occasionally. While doing these progressions, also substitute life rewards such as throwing a ball to him as a reward, letting him go outside as a reward, etc. in the training process.

🦴 **Your Attitude:** Keep your demeanor light and fun and your voice friendly and conversational, not demanding. Your dog "reads" your energy and your affect directly affects your dog's motivation to learn.

🦴 **Keep training sessions short:** Fifteen seconds to five minute sessions are ideal.

🦴 **The Forty-Five-Second Rule:** When you add the vocal cue in step 2 of the training process, say the word, such as "sit," only once and then wait up to forty-five seconds for a response. Do not say the vocal cue again. Sometimes it takes a dog that long to figure out what you want. By waiting for up to forty-five seconds, you may just give him the chance to be successful. If your dog won't do what you ask him to do within forty-five seconds, go back to the step in the training process where he's successful.

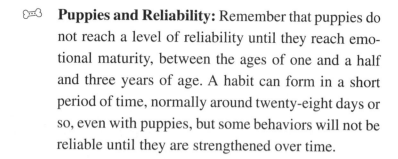 **Puppies and Reliability:** Remember that puppies do not reach a level of reliability until they reach emotional maturity, between the ages of one and a half and three years of age. A habit can form in a short period of time, normally around twenty-eight days or so, even with puppies, but some behaviors will not be reliable until they are strengthened over time.

If Your Dog Is Distressed

Some dogs won't eat or drink anything if they're distressed. This lack of eating or drinking is called inhibition. My dog Buck, for example, who was abused before he came to live with me, won't eat or drink all day if I'm gone. This behavior is rooted in a primal survival technique. In effect, Mother Nature is saying to the dog, "Don't eat anything! You can't afford to use your energy digesting food. You need all of your energy to stay alert for 'fight or flight.'" If you have such a dog, it's important to call a professional dog trainer who can show you step by step how to help your dog gain confidence and learn to relax.

Life Rewards

If your puppy or dog has a powerful inclination to sniff every bush and mark every tree, use those desires as rewards and make them part of your training instead of using food treats as rewards. Here's an example: Let's say you're teaching your dog to heel. The first step might be to just get your dog to sit for a second and say, "Okay! Go sniff!" In this situation, instead of giving your dog a food treat, you've given him permission to do what he really wants to do, which is sniff every blade of grass on the street. Then gradually progress, step by step, by having your dog walk by your side a step or two ("heel"), then have him sit again, and then once again release him to sniff. Then progress to having him walk a few more steps, having him sit, and releasing him again, and so on. Eventually he'll walk all the way around the block in heel position because he knows that at the end of the walk he can sniff to his heart's desire. This same process of teaching your dog to heel can be used with a dog who likes to fetch. You'd have him sit, then throw the ball, then walk a few steps and have him sit, and then throw the ball, and so on. Within a very short time, a dog learns that as long as he stays by your side when you ask him to do so, he eventually gets what he really wants, whether it be the freedom to sniff things or the freedom to chase a ball.

Here are some more examples of life rewards that can be used to shape specific behaviors:

- **Sit:** When your dog sits by the door, it opens to the backyard.
- **Down:** When your dog lies down, he's then allowed on the bed.
- **Go to Your Spot:** When your dog goes to his bed, you put his leash on to go for a walk.

⌐¤⌐   **Fetch:** When your dog gets you a soda or beer out of the fridge, you then throw his ball into the pool or the backyard.

Pay Attention

The first behavior I suggest teaching is pay attention because to motivate your dog to do what you ask, when you ask, you have to get her attention. If you think about it, your puppy or dog already pays attention whenever you pick up the leash, start to prepare her dinner, open the door to go outside, and so on. Without actually training her to "pay attention," you have established that behavior because she knows that something good is going to happen and looks to you. Now your goal is to purposefully teach your dog to pay attention so she will respond whenever you want her to.

To get your dog to pay attention to you whenever you ask, follow these steps:

Step 1. Get the behavior. Place a food treat in your hand and hold it in front of your dog's nose. In a smooth gesture, move your hand to your eyes and say "watch" or "pay attention" or "look." As your dog's eyes follow your hand going up to your face, praise and give the treat. Repeat these steps.

Step 2. Add the word (vocal signal). When you are 80 percent sure your dog will follow your hand motion, you are ready for the next step. Now, to be sure that your dog is following the signal, rather than being bribed by the food, put the treat in your other hand. Place your empty hand in front of your dog's nose and repeat as above, using the same marker word such as "look" as you move your hand to your eyes. Praise and treat from the hand that's holding the treat. Repeat.

Step 3. Use the word (vocal signal) only. When you are 80 percent sure your dog will follow the vocal cue only, begin to "fade" the hand signal. Gradually shorten the movement you are using from the dog's nose to the eyes, to just pointing to your eyes, and, finally, to using no movement at all.

Step 4. Add the 3D's. To increase reliability, progress by including the 3D's—longer duration, greater distance, and more distractions. Do not proceed too fast. Build on incremental success. If you've asked your dog to do something and he was unsuccessful twice, go back to a point where he was successful and build the behavior from there. Go back to using a treat as a lure if necessary whenever a new element is introduced in the behavior.

Hint

To speed this process: Face your dog. Put a treat in your hand and stretch your arm straight out from your side, parallel to the floor. Your dog will look at your hand. Now wait. Within forty-five seconds, your dog will turn her attention away from your hand and glance at your eyes. When she does, immediately praise and give her the treat. Repeat this five to ten times. When your dog figures this out, she will look at you as soon as you extend your hand. You can now add the words, "pay attention."

Figure 11-2

[Photo: a person kneeling on the floor holding a treat in front of a puppy's nose]

In step 1 of the pay attention behavior, put
a food treat in your hand and hold that
hand in front of your puppy's nose.

Figure 11-3

Then move the treat from the puppy's
nose to your eyes.

Sit

Step 1. Get the behavior. Always begin in an environment that has few or no distractions.

Place a highly valued food treat between your thumb and index finger. With your dog in front of you, move the hand that's holding the treat over the top of his nose until it's two inches or so from his head. Go no farther back than the crown of his head. The goal is to get your dog to tilt his head upward and look up at your hand. As he looks up, his back end will automatically go down, into the "sit" position. Encourage him by saying "goooood dog," "you're the best," "way to go," or the phrase of your choosing in a friendly but not too exuberant voice. As soon as his behind hits the floor, treat and praise! Then get your dog to move by throwing a treat and saying "Find it" so you can repeat this step. Repeat these steps five to ten times in each training session.

If you're having a problem with step 1 of sit:

- Perhaps you're holding the treat too far over his head, causing him to back up, *or* moving your hand too high, causing him to have to jump to get the treat, *or* moving your hand too low, causing him to nibble at your hand. Reread the instructions above and try again.

- Use approximations by rewarding every behavior that leads to sitting, such as looking up, leaning back, or the rear end almost touching the floor, which are all steps in the process of sitting. After every successful part of the behavior, reward your puppy or dog and gradually ask for more the next time.

Step 2. Add the word (vocal signal). When you are 80 percent sure your dog will sit whenever you begin to move your hand, begin saying "sit" just before you move your hand. Repeat five to ten times and proceed to step 3.

Step 3. Use the word (vocal signal) only. Now you're going to give the vocal signal by saying "sit" without first moving your hand. Keep your hands on your chest, say "sit," and wait. (This is the forty-five-second game; you're giving your dog forty-five seconds to figure out what you want.) If your dog doesn't sit within forty-five seconds and seems distracted, repeat step 2.

Do three to five sessions a day with about fifteen repetitions of each behavior for up to two or three minutes. Also be sure to incorporate the newly formed sit behavior in your dog's daily routine: At the door before going outside and before coming inside, up and down the stairs, before being let out of her kennel, and so on. In these examples, don't give treats as rewards; your dog's reward is the freedom to be with you.

To increase reliability, progress by including the 3D's—longer duration, greater distance, and more and more distractions. Do not proceed too far, too fast. Take baby steps and build on incremental success. If you've asked your dog to do something and he was unsuccessful two times, go back to a point where he was successful and build the behavior from there. Go back to using a treat as a lure if necessary whenever a new element is introduced in the behavior.

Figure 11-4

In step 1 of "sit" put a treat in your hand and slowly move it a few inches over the top of your dog's nose.

Figure 11-5

When the dog's behind hits the floor, praise and treat.

Lie down

Always begin in an environment that has few or no distractions.

Start with your dog in a sit position.

Step 1. Get the behavior

Hold a treat in your hand. Present the hand that's holding the treat just under your dog's nose and then move it straight to the ground—from the "nose to toes." As you do this, imagine that there's an invisible string connecting your hand and your dog's nose and you're pulling her nose to the ground. The moment she lies down, praise and treat. Repeat five to ten times.

Step 2. Add the word (vocal signal). When your dog is 80 percent reliable at lying down whenever you present the hand signal, say the word "down" *immediately before* giving the hand signal. When your dog does this three times in a row within three seconds of being asked, proceed to step 3.

Step 3. Use the word (vocal signal) only. With your dog in a sit position, say "down." (Be sure to continue to keep holding your hands to your chest.) Wait up to forty-five seconds for your dog to do the behavior. Even if your dog gets up, wait the forty-five seconds because he may still get it and lie down. If he doesn't, repeat step 2.

To increase reliability, progress by including the 3D's—longer duration, greater distance, and more and more distractions. Do not proceed too far, too fast. Take baby steps and build on incremental success. If you've asked your dog to do something and he was unsuccessful two times, go back to a point where he was successful and build the behavior from there. Go back to using a treat as a lure if necessary whenever a new element is introduced in the behavior.

Figure 11-6

When teaching your dog to lie down, start with her in a sit position. Move the treat from her "nose to toes."

Figure 11-7

When your dog lies down, praise and treat.

Stay

Not all trainers teach "stay" behavior; some believe that since you've told your dog to sit or lie down, he should wait for you to say "Okay" or give some other vocal cue that will release him and allow him to move from that spot. In reality, I find that doesn't work because most people forget to release their dogs, so the dogs end up releasing themselves. For that reason, I include the behavior "stay" in all exercises.

Remember, every exercise or behavior has a start and a finish. If you have asked your dog to stay in any position, you must remember to "end" the behavior and give a signal that releases your dog. If you forget to release your dog from a stay, she will eventually just release herself and leave. This makes for really unreliable stays.

I use the word "okay" as a release word, although some trainers feel the word "okay" is used so often in our daily vocabulary that the dog might hear the word somewhere in the environment and take off. You can say "find it," "that'll do," "thank you," "you're free," or whatever word you like to end the behavior and release your dog.

Step 1. Get the behavior. Ask your dog to sit or lie down; then, from the starting position of both hands on your chest, move your hand toward your dog, your palm facing your dog and back to your chest. Take a step back away from your dog and immediately return. If your dog doesn't move, praise and treat. Repeat five to ten times.

Step 2: Add the word (vocal signal). Say "stay" and back away and return. Praise and treat.

Step 3: Use the word (vocal signal) only. From starting position, say "stay" without the hand signal and repeat step 2.

To increase reliability, progress by including the 3D's— longer duration, greater distance, and more and more distractions. Do not proceed too far, too fast. Take baby steps and build on incremental success. If you've asked your dog to do something and he was unsuccessful two times, go back to a point where he was successful and build the behavior from there. Go back to using a treat as a lure if necessary whenever a new element is introduced in the behavior.

Come When Called

Come is an extremely important behavior. If your puppy or dog runs into the street, you want him to stop whatever he's doing and run back to you as soon as you call him or give him the signal without even thinking about it. To form "come when called" as a reliable behavior, I overemphasize the importance of taking baby steps in the training process. Then the key is to do thousands of repetitions over a long period of time and build on success. But be sure to keep the sessions short.

Remember, the number one rule is: Never call your dog to you unless you are 80 percent sure she'll respond; don't say "come" if there's a chance she won't. Also, don't call your dog to you if you're going to yell at her or if you're leaving for the day. Doing so would teach your dog that the word "come" leads to a negative consequence; hence, she won't come when called. And, unless she's very reliable with come when called, never shout "come" if she's running away. If you do, one of two things often occurs: 1) the word "come" becomes irrelevant to your dog, or 2) your dog associates the word "come" with running in the opposite direction from you. (See The 80-Percent Rule on page 171.)

Preparation: Rub some turkey, chicken, or cheese on your fingers.

Step 1. Get the behavior. With your hands in starting position on your chest, bring the treat-smelly hand two inches in front of your dog's nose. As soon as he touches it, praise and reward with a treat from the other hand. Repeat five to ten times.

Step 2. Add the word (vocal signal). Say "come" immediately before presenting your hand. For each repetition, add an inch or two of distance. Your goal is to make it so your dog can't wait to see that magic hand so he can run over and touch it.

Step 3. Use the word (vocal signal) only. Before you proceed to this step, make sure you have a really reliable "touch your hand when you say come."

Use everyday opportunities to practice, such as meal time, when you take him outside, when you let him out of the kennel, while you're cooking dinner, etc. While on a walk, periodically repeat this exercise.

To increase reliability, progress by including the 3D's— longer duration, greater distance, and more and more distractions. Do not proceed too far, too fast. Take baby steps and build on incremental success. If you've asked your dog to do something and he was unsuccessful two times, go back to a point where he was successful and build the behavior from there. Go back to using a treat as a lure if necessary whenever a new element is introduced in the behavior.

Building on Successes

Remember: Dogs learn on a curve. They have good days and bad days, just like us. They need time to integrate what they've learned. Each day, begin each exercise at your dog's learning baseline, that is, his starting point. Build on success.

Figure 11-8

In come when called, begin by putting your hands in
starting position on your chest.

Figure 11-9

When your dog touches your hand with his nose,
praise and treat.

Figure 11-10

As you progress in teaching come when called,
continue to add distance.

Go to Your Spot

Go to your spot redirects your puppy or dog's attention. It can calm a nervous dog and distract him from activities you don't want him to do, making it a great behavior for problem-solving. It is useful when your dog barks at the mail carrier, nudges you while you're on the phone, races to the door when the doorbell rings, begs at the dinner table, or acts fearful about strangers working around the house. It's also a great behavior to teach a dog for safety reasons, such as whenever a baby or small child enters a room. You can take your dog's spot ("bed") on trips or to your relatives over the holidays and tell him to simply chill there for as long as you want.

These go-to-your-spot instructions are exactly the same as the instructions for teaching your dog to go to his bed, blanket, mat, kennel, den, go outside, get in the house, etc. Just be sure to pick a different word for each different location. For instance, you could refer to the spot as "bed" or "go to your spot," or "place," or "kitchen," etc., but whatever you pick, always use the same word or phrase for the spot. Going step by step, most dogs will pick up this behavior very quickly; for some it will take several short sessions. Don't rush it, keep the sessions short and stop each session on a high note. The protocol for teaching go to the kennel is the same as go to your spot; however if your dog hasn't yet been kennel trained and is timid or fearful of the kennel, you'll want to use the special protocol on page 197 so he'll love being in his kennel.

Prepare: Stand beside the place you want your dog to use as a "spot" and make sure you are no more than one foot away from it. Start with your dog in a sit position facing you. Put your hands in the starting position on your chest.

Step 1. Get the behavior. Get the behavior using a treat (lure) and a hand signal. Let your dog see you throw a $10,000 treat onto the spot. The hand that is throwing the treat is the hand that is closest to the spot (Figure 11-11). For this behavior, the hand pointing to the spot and then immediately returning to your chest is the hand signal for go to your spot. As soon as your dog gets to the spot to get the treat, praise enthusiastically. (Figure 11-12) Repeat several times. When teaching go to your spot, you already know that your dog will take the treat that's offered. Since the rule is that you go to step 2 when you are 80 percent sure your dog will be successful, you can now proceed to step 2.

Figure 11-11

In step one of "go to your spot," start with your dog in a sit position facing you. Put your hands in the starting position on your chest.

Figure 11-12

Next, let your dog see you throw a $10,000
treat onto the "spot."

Step 2. Add the word (vocal signal). Attach a word to the
behavior along with the hand signal. Say "spot" (or other
word you've chosen) and throw the treat onto the "spot"
using the same hand motion you used in step 1. (Your hand
started on your chest, you threw the treat, and your hand
returned to your chest.) As soon as your dog touches the
spot, praise enthusiastically. Repeat five to ten times.

Progress to putting the treat in your other hand. Give the
verbal request and *pretend* to throw the treat, using the same
motion with the now empty hand (from your chest and back
again). Praise enthusiastically and then give your dog a treat
when he goes to the spot. The difference here is that you're no
longer using the treat as a lure or target. It is now used only as
a reward after your dog actually goes to the spot. When your
puppy or dog does the behavior within three seconds and is

able to repeat that behavior three times in a row, you're ready to go to step 3.

Step 3. Use the word (vocal signal) only. Use the word only without the hand signal. Keep your hands on your chest. Say the word once. Wait up to forty-five seconds. If your dog puts a paw on the spot, effusively praise and jackpot by giving him several treats. Repeat five to ten times. If your dog doesn't go to his spot within forty-five seconds, return to step 2. When your puppy or dog does the behavior successfully within three seconds and is able to repeat that behavior three times in a row, you're ready to go to step 4.

For shy or hesitant dogs, praise the smallest approximation of the behavior. In this case, reward your dog when he looks at the spot, then reward your dog when he takes one step toward the spot, then reward your dog when he puts one paw on the spot, and so on.

Step 4: Add Distance. Now you'll add distance by moving away from the spot, a foot at a time. Start two feet away from the spot. Say "Spot" and praise and treat every success. With each subsequent attempt, increase your distance from the spot. Continue to praise and reward every success. If your dog gets confused, it's a good bet you've gone too far too fast. Go back to the distance you were successful and work at that distance a little while longer. When your puppy or dog does the behavior within three seconds and is able to repeat that behavior three times in a row, you're ready to go to step 5.

Once you have begun to move farther from the bed (adding distance) you never throw the treat as a lure again. You only use the vocal signal. The only time you used the treat as a lure was at the very first step when you were next to the bed. After that, the treat is only used as a reward.

Step 5: Add Distractions. Once you've reached a point where your dog will go to her spot from virtually anywhere, add a distraction, like someone knocking at the door. To do this, go back to standing right by the spot and begin the training process all over. For example:

1. Stand by the door and send your dog to his spot. Praise and treat each success. Repeat five to ten times.
2. Next, knock or ring the door bell and immediately send your dog to his spot. Praise and treat each success. Repeat ten times. On the eleventh time, knock or ring the bell and say nothing. Wait up to forty-five seconds.

The signal of the knock on the door or ringing doorbell has now been installed as a signal for your dog to run to his spot. With several days, weeks, and months of practice, your dog will automatically go to his spot whenever someone knocks on the door or rings the doorbell. When your puppy or dog does the behavior within three seconds and is able to repeat that behavior three times in a row, you're ready to go to step 6.

Step 6: Gradually Add More Distance and Wean off Treats. As your dog is more successful with go to your spot, gradually add more distance and, over time, wean her off the treats by incorporating the intermittent reward schedule. Give her a treat every other time, then every third or fourth time, etc. In addition to food rewards, include life rewards such as going for a walk or a ride. "Want to go outside? Go to your bed first." Once he has really got it, you can wean him off treats and his reward can be simply getting to meet someone at the door, going for a ride, or anything else he really likes.

Hint

For this and all exercises that require your dog to move, your attitude can help tremendously. If it's fun for you, it's fun for your dog. So if your dog stands around or seems bored, get happy! Dance around; use different vocal sounds from kissy sounds to howls. Pretend to eat food and exaggerate with "hmmmmmm . . . look what I have!"

Then you're ready to add additional locations. Identify each location with its own individual "label" such as "bed," "mat," "kennel," "kitchen," "couch," etc. Work on these one at a time so each behavior is in place before you teach your dog to go to another place. For every new location, you must start from square one again.

Once your dog knows two or more different locations such as the bed and the kennel, you can then teach him to discriminate between them. To begin, put them at opposite ends of the same room and follow these steps:

1. Stand in the middle between the two objects and ask your dog to go to the bed. Reward every success. Then repeat ten times.
2. Still standing in the middle, send him to the kennel. Reward every success. Repeat that ten times.
3. Now, with voice only, say the word for one of the locations. See what happens.
4. When your dog goes to the location you've signaled at least 80 percent of the time, start moving one of the objects, such as the bed, closer to the other object along the circumference of the circle, so that you are still equal distance from the objects. For example, one location can now be in front of you and the other location is still off to your side.
5. Gradually build on success until the objects are next to each other.
6. Once your dog has this two-item behavior figured out, add the third item such as the mat. Repeat the whole

process, starting with the mat on the opposite side of
the room.

Having Problems?

🦴 Relax your expectations. It isn't necessary for your
dog to get it in one session.

🦴 Leave treats on the bed (or wherever) throughout the
day. Within a very short time, your dog will actually go to the spot and search for the treat. When
that happens, use the Magnet Game. Instantly praise,
and throw an extra treat to your dog the moment he
places a paw on the spot (or kennel, bed, etc.).

🦴 Because dogs have a tendency to follow your gaze,
make sure that you are looking at the spot you want
your dog to go to after giving the signal and not looking at your dog.

🦴 Make sure you wait a full forty-five seconds for your
dog to figure out what you want.

**Using Go to Your Spot to Teach Your Puppy or Dog
to Go to the Kennel**

Dogs have an innate dislike of being confined or
restrained so it's important to introduce the kennel gradually by associating it with safety and great things like food
treats. Teaching Go to the Kennel is taught exactly the same
as Go to Your Spot. However, don't close the gate until you
know your dog is comfortable being in the kennel. If the
kennel is the type that is enclosed, take the top off before
teaching this behavior.

Use Counter-Conditioning to Acclimate Your Dog to the Kennel

First, change the way your dog feels about the kennel by using counter-conditioning:

- 🦴 Lay a bunch of treats just inside the kennel door and, at each feeding time, make a line of treats going farther back into the kennel until, after a week, she has to go all the way inside to eat. It's important not to close the kennel gate during this process.
- 🦴 Sneak a great treat in the kennel when she's not looking and let her find it on her own. Whenever you notice that she's found and eaten the treat, sneak more treats into the kennel one at a time so she begins to associate the kennel as a magic treat-dispensing haven.

Once you realize that your dog is looking at the kennel as a positive place and starts to explore it without being asked to do so, start using the magnet game. That is, every time you see her going in the kennel, praise and throw her a treat.

Now you can start to teach her to go to her kennel using the Go to Your Spot protocol above.

1. Once you are sure she is comfortable going into the kennel, send her to the kennel and close the gate for one second. Immediately give her a treat through the gate.

Then open the gate and let her out. Repeat this three to five times, opening the gate immediately after treating.

2. Gradually progress to keeping the gate closed for longer periods of time for up to fifteen seconds, adding a second at a time before giving her a treat. This may take several sessions over days, weeks, or even months depending on your dog's sensitivity. When she's comfortable with the gate being closed for fifteen seconds, go to step 3.

3. Begin to add distance by moving away from the kennel and returning to it a step at a time. In other words, send your dog to the kennel, close the gate, back up one step, come forward one step, give your dog a treat, and open the gate. Each time you increase your distance from the kennel and return to your dog, give a treat and then open the gate again. Progress to the point where you leave the room for short periods of time and gradually increase to longer periods.

If you are training a young puppy, confinement won't be as much of a problem as that issue doesn't get triggered until a dog is a few months old. Puppies are more adaptable and accept things as they are more easily. That being said, every dog is an individual and, if your puppy is having extreme difficulty with being confined, don't confine him. Call a professional dog trainer for advice.

Leave It

"Leave it" means: "Dog, don't touch whatever you are eye-ing." This could be the Thanksgiving turkey, your shoes, the children's stuffed animals, the remote (God-forbid), his poop, road kill, or my Portuguese Water Dog's favorite—dead fish. You can also use "leave it" to keep your dog from approaching other dogs, cats, and people.

Step 1: Get the behavior. Put a treat on the floor and cover it with your hand. Your dog will probably sniff your hand and paw at it for up to a minute. The instant your dog pulls her nose away, even an inch, uncover the treat. As soon as your dog goes for the treat, cover it up again. After several repetitions of this, your dog will have a "wait a minute, something's happening here" moment and hesitate instead of going for the treat. If he hesitates for even a fraction of a second and doesn't go toward the treat, immediately praise him and then give him the treat. In this behavior, you are rewarding your dog for not approaching the treat. Repeat this five to ten times. Now proceed to step 2.

Step 2: Attach a Word to the Behavior and Add Duration (More Time). Say "leave it," then put the treat on the ground with your hand on top of it, and then uncover the treat and reward him with praise and give him the treat for not coming forward. Now progress to uncovering the treat and having him wait for longer periods of time—first for two seconds, then three, etc. Once your dog will leave the treat for ten seconds, go to step 3.

Figure 11-13

In step 1 of "Leave It," put the treat on the floor or ground and cover it with your hand.

Figure 11-14

Continuing step 1 of "Leave It," uncover the treat the instant your dog pulls his head away. If your dog hesitates for even a fraction of a second and doesn't go toward the treat, immediately praise him and then give him the treat. If he does go toward the treat, cover it up again.

Figure 11-15

In step 2 of "Leave It" you will progress to saying "Leave It," uncovering the treat and then
having your dog wait—first for two seconds,
then three, etc. before praising him and giving him the treat. Once your dog will leave
the treat for ten seconds, go to step 4.

Step 3. Add Distance. Say "leave it" and then drop the
treat on the floor (instead of placing it) from a height of
two inches off the floor. If your dog goes toward the treat,
quickly cover it. If he hesitates and doesn't go toward the
treat, praise him and give him the treat that you dropped.
Progress to increasing the distance you drop the treat to
three inches, four inches and so on until you can drop the
treat from a standing position. Then proceed to step 4.

Step 4. Add More Distance. Next, increase the distance
between you and your dog. Say "leave it,'" drop the treat,
take one step away, return and praise, and give your dog
the treat that you dropped. Then say "leave it," then drop
it and move two steps away, return, and so on.

Hints for Teaching "Leave It"

Do not release your dog and allow her to get the treat herself. Always pick up the treat that you dropped and then give it to your dog. This method will really help when you accidentally drop a piece of food on the kitchen floor. Your dog will have a powerful habit installed that she can never touch something unless you give it to her.

If your puppy or dog tries to steal food from the table or kitchen counter before she becomes reliable with leave it, interrupt the behavior. Do this by startling her with a sound intense enough to get her to stop what she's doing and get her back on all fours. Whistle, shake a can, or clap loudly, etc.—but startle, don't scare! Then do three practice "leave its" to remind her that she'll be given the treats if she lies down and waits. Until your dog figures this out, use the prevention and management tools of tethers or baby gates to keep her from stealing food and hence being self-reinforced!

Heeling

Heeling means your puppy or dog walks or stands by your side within an imaginary boxed area by your leg—not too far ahead of you, not too far behind you, not too far from your side, and not too close to you. The idea is that he stays within the perimeters of this imaginary box, without bumping your leg. Even puppies can learn how to heel within a couple of days. That being said, reliable heeling normally occurs when a dog reaches emotional maturity between the ages of one and four. As with other behaviors, reliability with heeling means that your dog will do the behavior with all sorts of distractions.

Heeling doesn't follow the usual three-step process (get the behavior, add the word, then use the word only). Your dog will figure this out quickly; therefore, because you are already 80 percent sure your dog will be successful in doing the behavior, there is no need for step one. Here are two methods for teaching heeling. Try them both and see which works best for you.

Heeling—Method 1: The Traditional No-Force Method

Steps 1 and 2: Get the behavior and attach a word.
In a nondistracting environment, have your dog sit by your side. With your hands in starting position on your chest, say "heel" and, using the hand that is closest to your dog, stick a treat in her mouth. Do not walk forward while you do this. Stay in one place and don't move. Repeat this five to ten times. The hand signal for heel is similar to the hand signal for come. Your hand will move from your chest down to your side. This works because both come and heel are targeting behaviors. In other words, wherever the target hand is, that's where your dog is supposed to be. The only difference

between come and heel is that in the come behavior your dog is coming toward you and facing you. In the heel behavior your dog is facing the same direction as you.

Step 3: Add motion. Your dog will now be looking up at your hand anticipating another treat. At this point, begin to walk. While walking, say the word "heel" and simultaneously stick a treat in your dog's mouth. As you continue to walk, each time you say "heel," the hand next to your dog brings the treat from your chest to your dog's mouth. Repeat five to ten times.

Step 4: Say the word only. Keep your hands on your chest. Say the word "heel" one time and begin walking. Take four or five steps, then stop and say "sit." (Use the sit hand signal—hand up over the dog's head—if you need to.) When your dog sits, praise, and then give her the treat. Begin again and each time gradually add more steps before stopping and asking your dog to sit. For example, take eight or nine steps, then ask your dog to sit. Then twelve or thirteen, and so on. Whenever you come to a stop, praise and treat. If you practice this heeling exercise and add the distance of one additional house-length each day, you'll be around the block in a month or two with your dog remaining in heel position.

Figure 11-16

Step 1 of heeling: With your dog by your side, say "heel" and
simultaneously stick a treat in her mouth.

Figure 11-17

Step 3 of heeling: Begin to walk with your dog by your side. Say "heel" and simultaneously stick a treat in her mouth while walking.

Figure 11-18

Step 4 of heeling: Keep your hands on your chest, say "heel," and walk with your dog. Take four or five steps, stop, ask your dog to sit, and then give her a treat.

208

Method 2: Spontaneous Heeling

This method is a variation of The Magnet Game (see page 75). It is so easy that the three-step training process does not apply to this method.

Step 1.

In a nondistracting environment, meander around an enclosed area or yard with your dog off the leash. If you don't have an enclosed area in which to work, put him on a twenty-foot leash so he can't wander off.

Step 2.

Whenever your dog happens to walk by your side, praise and treat. You can encourage (prompt) him to do this more and more often by patting your leg, taking quick little steps, and praising even the slightest interest in staying by your side. Every time he starts going off in another direction, you should abruptly turn and go the other way, being careful, of course, not to jerk him if he's on lead. Every time he happens to come up to your side, once again, praise and treat. If he stays there, continue to praise and treat.

Hints for Beginning Heeling

- Make sure your dog has had plenty of exercise before teaching heeling.
- Keep the sessions short.

Having problems?

- **For a dog who won't stay by your side:** If your dog wants to come in front of you when you stop, that is natural as she's used to getting rewards while standing in front of you for all the other behaviors. To resolve this, bring the treat close to her nose as you prepare to stop. *As you stop*, use the sit hand signal: Bring the treat slightly over her head and then give it to her when she sits. If you repeat this five to ten times, that should solve the problem.

- **If your dog is disinterested:** Your attitude can really help. Continually praise your dog and keep an upbeat attitude while training.

- **Try the "horse-feedback" trick:** If you think your dog is going to get really distracted by something or someone, the "horse feedbag" trick is often helpful when teaching heeling. Put a bunch of treats in your hand and, as you walk your dog past the distractions, allow your dog to nibble the treats from your hand. She will then be happily eating the food from your hand and the distractions will be less significant to her. This is an especially good thing to do when you are walking your dog past houses and yards with barking dogs who go nuts whenever you pass by.

- **If lunging is a problem:** As vigilant as we are in trying not to jerk our dogs or put them in the position of jerking themselves, there are times when your dog will simply lunge forward, such as when he tries to chase a squirrel or another dog. In these emergencies, you must have the ability to stop him. This is another good reason to use the bungee leash and an anti-pulling harness to minimize the chances of your dog escaping or hurting himself.

If pulling is a problem: If your dog is pulling and he is one of those extra powerful dogs or if he was abused before you got him—as is the case with many rescue dogs—it may be helpful to use an Easy Walker or halter-style collar with these methods. The combination of an anti-pulling collar with a bungee leash, often gives 50 percent more control of your dog immediately.

Heeling—Advanced Level

Once your dog is successful at heeling using one of the methods above, it's time to add the 3D's—longer duration, distance, and distractions. Here are some ways to do that:

1. Ask a friend to stand ten or fifteen feet away from you and your dog. With your dog in heel position, walk up to the person and have your dog sit. Then shake the person's hand and ask the person to walk away. Praise and reward your dog.

2. Repeat the previous step with this difference. This time you and your dog will stay in position and your friend will approach you. The other person walks up to you, shakes your hand, and walks away. Praise, and reward.

3. Start at a distance of about thirty feet from another person. With your dog in heel position, walk toward the other person as the other person walks toward you. When you meet, have your dog sit, then shake hands with the other person. Then you and the other person should continue to walk in opposite directions. As you are walking, praise and treat.

Hints for Advanced Heeling

- Start with a person your dog knows and have her say hello to your dog before practicing.
- If your dog gets up each time the person approaches, keep your foot on the leash.

Conclusion

We humans are great! Using our unlimited creativity, intelligence, intuition, imagination and willpower, we've figured out how to reach the moon, find cures for diseases, and build dams that create power for millions of people. In addition to all this, our unlimited capacity for kindness and compassion has resulted in humanitarian efforts that feed and care for millions of people and animals. I believe we all can attain whatever we want in life by remembering to tap into that unlimited source of compassion that's inside each of us and, by so doing, solve even our most demanding problems. It is this capacity for greatness, this coupling of mind and heart, that creates the ideal environment for raising the family dog.

One of the animal shelters where I work and volunteer places great emphasis on finding the right animal for each person or family and then educating that person or family to maximize the potential for a successful outcome. Those who wish to adopt a dog are required to attend a one-and-a-half hour pet-parenting class with the director of the shelter and then another hour with me to learn about basic canine behavior. Wouldn't it be terrific if all shelters mandated such an educational program? How many people and dogs would be helped in making the transition from shelter to home easier, as well as increase the odds that the new family will live happily-ever-after?

As I've said throughout this book, it is much more fun to educate a dog when training becomes a habit rather than a chore. It is my hope that the methods and tools presented herein will assist everyone with their dog-human communication skills, and thereby eliminate behavior problems and help lead us all to a happier and more peaceful world.

Free Online Video Seminar

You've read the book—now watch the video to see the practices you learned to use in this book!

A free 60-minute online video seminar is exclusively available to thank you for purchasing this book, *The Dog Whisperer Presents: Good Habits for Great Dogs*. This unique book and online video package provide a comprehensive learning experience in which Paul Owens shares concepts which, until now, have been available only to his clients via in-person classes. You will see Paul in action as he presents his revolutionary new "habit training" methods which are destined to become the standard for positive dog training all over the world for decades to come.

To access this unique training seminar, visit *www.Dog WhispererDVD.com/habits* and enter your password. The password is the first three words on page 110, with no spaces.

By visiting the site and entering the password, you'll be treated to demonstrations of:

- ⊱ The unique and revolutionary 7-day Vacation for Canine Education program.
  - The 7-day Vacation teaches people how to understand dogs and speak their language in the quickest way possible. On the video, you will see for yourself just how easy the 7-Day Vacation is and why it is so effective. You'll learn to play games that reinforce good behaviors with your dog. These fun and easy games consist of the Find-it trilogy and the five Magnet Game Behaviors, which are taught without signals or commands—sit, down, look, going to the bed, and bringing a toy to you.
- ⊱ The proper use of tethering for safety and positive training.
  - Paul addresses the safety of both the dog and the human family by demonstrating how to temporarily tether (tie up) a dog in such a way that the dog loves the experience. Then, as the dog quickly learns what to do using Paul's "habit training" methods, with no need for physical punishment or corrections, tethering can be discontinued.
- ⊱ Self-help for both people and dogs and methods to easily correct problem behaviors.
  - This is the first dog training program to address how to motivate both dogs and humans. A segment on the video will address tips and instructions on how you

can motivate your dog to happily do what is asked, as well as how to motivate yourself to train and play with your dog.

🦴 Easy ways to correct troublesome problem behaviors.

- Paul's revolutionary 28-day "habit training" program will teach you to easily correct troublesome problem behaviors such as barking, whining, digging, chewing, biting, jumping, and so on. Paul demonstrates these principles on the video using both puppies and dogs so you can see for yourself how effective and powerful the methods really are.

So what are you waiting for? Visit *www.DogWhisperer DVD.com/habits*, enter the password (the first three words of page 110 with no spaces), and enjoy this invaluable seminar hosted by Paul Owens—the original Dog Whisperer!

Index

Page numbers in *italics* indicate figures

Also from Paul Owens ...

DVDs and lots of free advice and video clips at <u>www.DogWhispererDVD.com</u>

The *Dog Whisperer DVD - Vol. 1*
Beginning & Intermediate Dog Training for Puppies and Dogs

"The best DVD on basic training & highly recommended."

— *Chronicle of the Dog* (The journal of professional dog trainers)

"Paul Owens is hands-down the BEST dog trainer I have ever worked with."

— *Jeff Probst, host of TV's "Survivor"*

The Dog Whisperer DVD - Vol. 2
Solving Common Behavior Problems for Puppies and Dogs (2-disc Program)

"Renowned dog trainer Paul Owens hosts this informative program explaining how to effectively deal with problematic dog behaviors. Hoping to dispel the common misconceptions about dealing with dogs, Owens explains the simple but important changes that most dog owners can make to get results, stop bad behaviors, and keep the furriest member of their family both well behaved and happy."

— *Cammila Albertson, All Movie Guide*